FROM GOD TO CLIMATE CHANGE

The journey of Albert's 30-year mission in China to
scientist son Ben's fight with the riddle of the world

Tony Garnier

Published by Tony Garnier 2022
Publishing Partner: Paragon Publishing, Rothersthorpe

ISBN 978-1-78222-969-8

Book design, layout and production management by Into Print
www.intoprint.net
+44 (0)1604 832149

This book is dedicated to my grandfather, the late Albert John Garnier, whom I never met. He sparked an interest for me to travel on the journeys related in this book and to rediscover my heritage and father, the late Benjamin John Garnier.

Contents

INTRODUCTION

Albert Garnier, 1952.

My grandfather, Alberto Giovanni Garnier, a Waldensian Italian who in 1948 became Albert John Garnier and a British citizen, was an influential Protestant (Baptist) missionary to China for 30 years.

Between 1906 and 1936, Albert, or Chia Liyan (賈立言) as Chinese named him, was known to millions through his many radio talks and publications. His books included *A Maker of Modern China, The Planting of Christianity,* and especially *Chinese versions of the Bible,* reported to have had a circulation of a million copies. As secretary of the Shanghai-based Christian Literature Society, in 1933 he was instrumental in founding a religious radio station, from which he frequently broadcast across China.

If, as some authorities claim, a Protestant-styled spiritual resurgence is underway in modern-day China, linked to rapidly rising living standards, the influence of Albert Garnier and colleagues must be acknowledged.

My father, Benjamin John Garnier, in contrast, did not believe in the existence of God, the Creator. Ben was a scientist. As a climatologist, he stressed the damage to Earth of human-induced climate change, decades before the rest of the world woke up to it. Over 40 years of reading and writing he believed that the solution to the world's problems resided squarely in the evolution of the human brain.

Ben sought to put mankind's questionable treatment of Earth into a 'scientific' holistic or global context, and understand WHY and WHAT could or should be done about it. He believed in the possibility of finding the truth himself. Thus, he could *learn,* he could grow in knowledge, even if he might never *know* – that is, know for certain.

That God, or any other authority, commands a person to do a certain thing is no guarantee that the command is right. It is 'I' who must decide whether to accept the standards of any authority as morally good or bad. Problems are created by people, and which people must necessarily solve. This is a core Waldensian idea, even though accepted by many people across numerous communities.

Ben noted the discovery that the human brain has evolved through three stages over the past three million years – 'reptilian' and 'limbic' (which we can call the 'old brain'), and the 'neocortex,' over the last half a million years, barely a second on the evolutionary time-scale. Why has learning to use our 'new' brains been so slow? The belief is that the 'old' brain got in the way of, or acted as a brake on the new.

All previous generations of mankind have had to come to terms with the prospect of his/her death as an individual. The present generation is the first to face the prospect of the death of our species (The Sixth Extinction). The most challenging issue facing mankind is, therefore, the problem of controlling man's reptilian (brain's) intolerance and struggle for territory, while at the same time finding a means of regulating our soaring population, moderating climate change and controlling the split between rational and irrational thinking, affecting basic beliefs that are threatening society's longevity.

Late in his life, Ben concluded that if he had his time again, instead of geography (and climatology) – advocating successfully, as he did in the 1940s and 1950s in several countries, that the subject be taught across the secondary school curriculum and university – he would recommend that learning how the brain works – biological order, mental creativity and behaviour – become a core subject at secondary school.

If there is anything 'good' in this analysis, Ben said, it is that young people are beginning to understand what is really happening. I am confident that Albert would agree too, not only for China, but for the world tomorrow.

I never met my grandfather, but in 1951 when I was aged 10, he began writing a bi-monthly letter from far-away London to me in New Zealand.

How that came about was to have been the main theme of this book – a Garnier family history dating from 1265, for the family. But research revealing Albert's action-packed 30-years in a rapidly transforming China, from a feudal, underdeveloped backwater to an active 'Belt and Road' economic, scientific and military superpower, and Ben's findings on our climate crises and observation on mankind's evolution of a brain which it does not know how to use properly, encouraged a change.

As important as were Albert's passion and love for China together with his anguished life through two world wars, I gradually came to appreciate the dominant role played in his interpretation of China through his own 700-years of Waldensian community ancestry in northern Italy, where he was raised, his extended family and his spiritual values – those of a Protestant liberal Christian who often quietly advised that 'prompt action, without fear, is the only way an opportunity, a problem, a challenge can be carried through.'

This book is intended to chronicle the growth of today's disorderly, threatened world through the life of the evolving ideas, values and deeds of Albert and his Waldensian relatives, and the influence they have carried to his son, my 'true' father, and myself.

Without my grandfather's letters and influence, this book would never have been written, and my life would have been, I am sure, dramatically different. To understand why and how it happened, we must visit the Waldensian village of Torre Pellice, in northern Italy, in the mid-1880s, where my grandfather's values and beliefs were forged and drove him to pursue an active, values-based life in the service of God (Mankind?) and selected individuals.

PROLOGUE

Gisborne, late-November 1952: An isolated coastal city on the East Coast of New Zealand's North Island, and the world's first to see the sun each day.[1] Enjoying another day of clear blue sky and hot Mediterranean-like weather, surfing at Waikanae Beach, a game of tennis, and arriving home, as usual around 4pm, I check for any mail. What's this? An airmail letter post-marked London, England, addressed to 'Anthony Garnier'.

It must be from a relative unaware that for the past two years I have become 'Tony,' doing away with fatherly affection names such as 'Ant' and 'Anthony Ant the Pirate.' For I have no father; He left two years ago, to take up a lecturing position at Ibadan University, Nigeria – leaving behind his wife (Rocky) and children (Anthony, 11 years; Christopher, 9 years; and, Susan, 4). Is the letter from my father? No.

The letter is from my grandfather, Grandpa Albert. He introduces himself as the father of Ben, my father, and knows that Ben moved to Nigeria without his family. Grandpa Albert lives in Sevenoaks, Kent and says he knows how angry I must be, a fatherless son, just as he was when aged just four his father, Giovanni Garnier, passed away after an illness and he was shipped off from Rome to live in a small stone house in far off Angrogna, Torre Pellice, 50km from Turin in the Cottian Alps close to the French and Swiss borders.

Some stamps were included from China and England. He must have been told that I had started collecting two years earlier, while at boarding school in Christchurch where Christopher and I were sent after my parents broke up.

The circumstances of my family's 'break-up' weren't mentioned, and never were in the 18-years of letters we exchanged. However, he is sensitive to me as, like himself, he tells me, I am a Garnier, a Waldensian Garnier; my ancestry is very important to him. But I failed to appreciate just how much store he puts in this until years later, 1975, when, at age 34, I visited his home town in northern Italy and began meeting relatives and researching my background. By then Albert had died.

My teenage life was disrupted. I refused to accept my mother's new husband, and I left 'home', angry and resentful, boarding with a pensioner looking for company and revenue, for my last months at secondary school and beginning a working life in Gisborne. It could have been as a carpenter's apprentice, having been proficient at woodwork at school, but ended up in the local Lands & Survey office learning to draft maps and become a land surveyor.

Albert's first letter came around the time I moved – just in time. In subsequent letters, he encouraged me to work out what I wanted to do with my life and get educated to be able to do it: "Perhaps the story of my boyhood failings may help you to avoid them" was his theme. But his message took time to sink in.

Albert's monthly or bi-monthly letters continued until 1970. Always encouraging, always positive, always quietly probing with stories about his youth, family and outlook on life.

He never discussed his theology, and said little about his 30 years in China and war-time experiences, the extent of which I only became aware of through a volume of writing he undertook and were passed to family members by Albert's daughter, Enrica, my aunt, after he died.

Through his letters I learn that Albert Garnier's family lived the simplest of lives. When his father died, Albert's mother, Fanny, was faced with bringing up four children in a small, isolated, Angrogna cottage. She made all the clothes. Albert told that sometimes even dry bread was short in the house, and that he missed a year of school because he was too disruptive and a reluctant participant.

Gradually Albert's influence grew and my time in Gisborne ended (after four years) as ambition shifted. Life's serious purpose had taken over. I had grown into a free-thinking youth, with an independent spirit, a loner, but committed to community values, lifelong learning and education, and economical balance. Years later, I learn that these traits are broadly the values of my Waldensian ancestors, but Albert never said as much or compelled me to adopt them.[2]

In two steps, I shift to Auckland to attend Auckland University, via a return to Dunedin for a year, where my father founded the Department of Geography at Otago University. Albert had wanted me to know that when I grew up, I would be judged not from my thinking or thoughts (beliefs), or fears but my actions. Even though I was a lazy student, and didn't study at high school, I knew I had a brain whose thinking tended towards promoting action and getting a result, based on logical outcomes, common sense and putting in a 100% effort.

Albert's last but one letter, 31 September 1968, six months after his wife of 50 years died, began in Chinese, praised my effort to learn the language.[3]

"Your Chinese letter makes me particularly happy. I am now old and from time to time face the risk of being unable to keep up with this new era. But the past has passed and it will never come back, all we have is today. I wonder if you are still a philatelist. My opportunity to collect

stamps is minimal now, but I still like to study all my Chinese stamps, in particular, those used for Air Mail issued in the 10th Republic (1921)."

In fact, I struggle through university, but am determined to succeed – eventually acquiring an MA in Philosophy with Chinese language in support. Still angry, while fellow students marched to protest the Vietnam War, for a reason I can't fathom, in 1970 I wrote my protest in an article and sent it to the local newspaper *The Auckland Star*. It was in response to an earlier article from someone, an adult, protesting at the anti-war campaigns of young Aucklanders. My article was published and became a significant signpost in my life going forward. Spread across a page as an 'outburst of opinion' at the adult generation's claim that modern youth 'make me tired,' my article pointed out that if you really want freedom and love and peace then, surely, it is time to relax and enjoy your 'freedom'.

"Grow up and realise that freedom is there not just to be worked for but to be enjoyed. Your 40 long years have made YOU tired! As you say, it is OUR turn. Why not OURS and YOURS? But you are tired. ... So, the best thing for you is to go QUIETLY to sleep. When someone's tired, then surely, it is time they went to sleep?" [4]

A job offer followed and I soon found myself in Wellington, at the Star's Press Gallery Office at Parliament. Parliamentary work consumed me. I was launched into a career based on word-smithing, winning a number of NZ Journalist Union awards for critical and investigative journalism and writing a weekly political column 'Weekwatch' for 10 years.

Through the mid-1970s and 1980s, two best-selling books were co-authored, *The Hunter and the Hill*, a study of Prime Minister Norman Kirk's years in politics, and, *Election '81: An End to Muldoonism?* an assessment of the record of the third National Government led by Sir Robert Muldoon. [5]

Tony Garnier.

At the conclusion of the 1981 Election Campaign, I asked Muldoon if the Springbok rugby tour had cost the Government three of its Wellington urban seats on election night, as he had indicated it might earlier in the campaign. He replied that "the damage" had been done by journalists "like Garnier consistently adopting anti-National viewpoints".

As I denied the allegation and suggested to the Prime Minister that I didn't think political journalists could be so influential, Muldoon snapped: "You just print what I say. That's all I ask, that's all I want." In the report of the incident, *The Evening Post* noted that I regard my job as a political correspondent as three-fold – to report what the politicians say, to explain what it means, and to criticize and praise where warranted.[6]

With little thought of my grandfather and the years of concern he had shown and influence exerted in correspondence he had sent through the 1950s and 1960s, numerous work-related trips to Australia, America, Asia, Africa and Europe followed. I took the opportunity to visit Torre Pellice, reconnect with my father Ben (by now head of the Geography Department at McGill University in Montreal), and visit China – twice, in 1984 and 1987.

My first visit to Torre Pellice was a sharp reminder of my debt to Albert. It was like 'coming home' and many subsequent visits have reinforced the sense of well-being that Torre Pellice gives me. Is it a genetic connection or the influence of my grandfather to help shape my outward-looking, trusting world-view? The like-mindedness with other Garniers and kinship with the Torre Pellice community prompt me to ask a question: Is there a genetic determinism connection in my make-up? Quite possibly.

My father, late-brother and cousin, Bristol-based Michael Garnier, all independently experienced a similar 'connection' of 'coming home' when they first visited Torre Pellice. And having raised it here, Michael sent me an article from the New Yorker titled *Querencia – A sense of belonging*[7] which Ben sent him after they'd discussed their mutual feeling of 'coming home' when they visited Torre Pellice.

'Querencia' is a Spanish word that means affection for the place one calls home and the sense of well-being that place gives one. It is an offshoot of the verb 'quere', to desire, and can be applied to the contentment of a wild animal in its haunts as well as the comfort felt by a person in familiar surroundings. It means that sense of being nourished by a place in which you belong. It means needing that place and having it. The article states a truism: *We live in a world awash with people torn from their 'querencia' who face the enormously difficult task of cultivating another. Once found, it cannot be lightly discarded, because lack of 'querencia' is a kind of starvation. 'Querencia' nurtures.*

In Torre Pellice I also discover the considerable research my father has undertaken to understand (and perhaps solve) the riddle of the world. And Albert may have been more perceptive than he could ever know, in the extent to which China's economic and spiritual revival may (or may not) affect the thinking and conduct of the future world. You be the judge. Ben and Albert's polar opposite lifestyle and thinking sits at the heart of the story that follows.

PART ONE: **MISSION CHINA**

Chapter 1: ALBERT'S CHINA INITIATION AT THE END OF THE QING DYNASTY (1644 – 1911)

THE grey, choppy China Sea rolls on, and the ship repeatedly pitches and keels.

It is towards the end of 1906 and 25-year-old Albert Garnier is aboard a German liner, Prince Rupert Lintgold, en route from Genoa to Shanghai. Albert is the sole new recruit in a group of missionary veterans returning to various parts of Asia. He is alone in heading for a missionary station in inland China, Taiyuan, the capital of Shanxi Province and part of the Qing Dynasty dating from the sixteenth century.[8]

The captain walks freely around the deck, berating the poor missionaries stretched out on their deck chairs feeling dreadfully sea-sick. "It's your own fault," he laughs, "all your prayers have driven a host of evil spirits off dry land, and now they're taking their revenge by throwing you about."

Everything is new for Albert: the Suez Canal, the Red Sea, the Indian Ocean, Singapore, Hong Kong and the China Sea, which is proving to be the roughest part of the month-long sea voyage.

From his teenage years, Albert has wanted to be a missionary in China. He still doesn't know why. As the ship bucks and heaves against the choppy seas, he thinks of his far away inland home on a mountain slope close to Torre Pellice in the Waldensian valleys in Northern Italy. The contrast could not be greater. Cut off from the plains by snow for weeks on end during the winter months, the steep valley sides drop precipitously into fast-flowing rivers. Lilies of the valley, convolvulus and juniper grow where the forest gives way to woods, and the villages below with their alpine houses and overhanging roofs.

It was here that in the 12th century a tight-knit, highly educated spiritual Waldensian community established. Comprising mainly French escaping from persecution, they were intent on learning the Gospels and holding themselves apart from conforming to the Catholic doctrine. Over 200 years they had established in the isolated mountainous valleys and hill sides, a strong and independent Protestant Waldensian Church looking spiritually towards England and Switzerland. In the sixteenth and seventeenth centuries they had resisted troops from Catholic Savoy in a series of valiant, brutal confrontations and expulsions. By the middle of the eighteenth century, the Waldensian Church had weathered the centuries as an enclave of liberalism, clothed in the 'spiritual armour' of its heroic history and keeping up strong links with foreign Protestantism. Its followers eventually became Italian citizens, but centuries of persecution had left them proud, rebellious, high-minded and combative for their faith. Weather and geography encouraged a tough mentality, a gift for survival.

Albert recalled that as a teenager he had become a proud non-commissioned officer in the Waldensian School's armed forces, tramped the Waldensian valleys of the Cottian Alps south-west of Turin on the Italian-French frontier, and seen where his heroic relatives had bravely fought – the valleys of Pellice, Germanasca, Angrogna, Luserna and the Chisone.

In the village of Torre Pellice, the Waldensian Church's headquarters, there is a large stone church, a boarding school and college, which Albert had attended and from which he emerged as a top student. Albert's father, Giovanni, had also been educated in Torre Pellice, and become head of a Waldensian faculty of theology in Rome, the city where Albert was born in 1881. He was a proud Waldensian, an Italian.

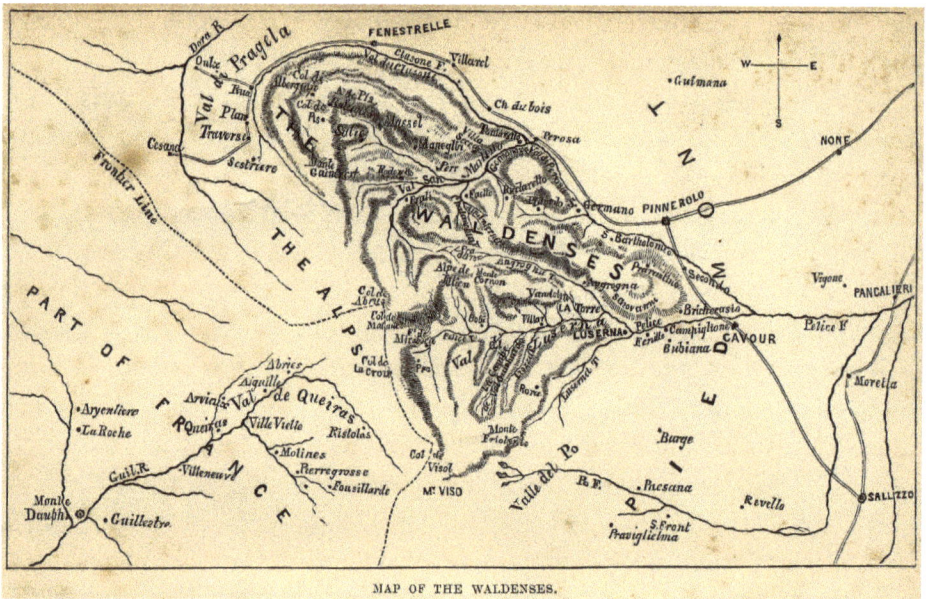

MAP OF THE WALDENSES.

Source: Alexis Muston, The Israel of the Alps, 1862.

As the ship approaches Shanghai, Albert briefly questions how he will manage. He has mastered six languages (French, Italian, Latin, Greek, Hebrew and English) but not Chinese. Of Chinese social structure and values, he knows little, other than that it has remained a united, inventive civilization for more than 5000 years, through many dynastic twists and turns.

Albert recalls that the French philosopher Voltaire had written: "One need not be obsessed with the merits of the Chinese to recognize that their empire is the best that the world has ever seen." [9] For much of the 18th and 19th centuries, that was the view basically everyone in Europe took. The meritocracy of Chinese civil service fascinated Europeans, while Chinese art was considered so perfect that Asian motifs started to appear in the work of a generation of European painters.

But what about recent history? The Taiping Rebellion that exploded in southern China in 1850 and over the next 14 years saw over 600 cities destroyed and a death toll upward of 20 million.

For a millennium the Chinese considered themselves to be at the centre of the universe insofar as the arts, civil administration and commerce were concerned. But from the mid-1800s, China was simply too weak to resist the demands for territorial concessions by European powers and Japan, who then proceeded to carve China into various spheres of influence for commercial and cultural exploitation, including by missionaries.[10]

But resistance to "foreign devils" had gradually developed, and the missionaries in Taiyuan had recently become prime targets. Albert was well aware that just six years earlier, "Boxer" militia bands began singling out Chinese Christians for persecution, then went after the missionaries themselves.

After more than a month at sea, landing in Shanghai was reassuring – a bustling, active port city, not unlike Genoa back in Italy. But the eight-day journey from Shanghai to the inland city of Taiyuan in northern China was a riveting wake-up, a trip back through time, giving Albert a stripped-down galaxy of images and cultural truths stretching from the Bronze Age and Tang Dynasty when China was the world's Central Kingdom.[11] The only means of transport available was an un-sprung wagon with large iron-rimmed wheels drawn by two mules that covered around 30 miles a day on average.

"I did the whole journey on foot," Albert recalled years later, "not only to avoid being jolted in the wagon, but also to enjoy the scenery." They would set out at dawn, but towards mid-day stop for three to four hours to rest both travellers and animals. The Chinese call that 'the long rest', but when Albert said it was a waste of time, the muleteer looked at him in amazement and said: "But, sir, if you have no time, what have you got?" For Albert it was an early confirmation of what he had been told before setting out: the Chinese are a philosophic race.

Each evening they would over-night at one of the huge inns located along the main highway. These comprised a large courtyard with rooms all around it, and sheds used as stables. "We would make a noisy entrance through the main gate, the muleteers whacking away with their whip-handles at their unfortunate beasts, wearied by the end of the day, meanwhile calling them everything under the sun. The more you clatter, the more you shout, the more you draw attention to the importance of the traveler."

There was no furniture in the rooms except a square table and one or two wooden chairs; everything else, the traveler was expected to provide, including the bed. A wadded quilt was stretched on the brick platform which occupied almost the whole room and below which a coal-fire was lit – a very economical form of central heating, but which could be dangerous because of the fumes from the coal. The warmth also roused a multitude of small creatures to whom the "raw recruit" had to accustom himself if he wanted to get some sleep, and then he was likely to be up before sunrise.

"I shall never forget the impression I had on the morning of the eighth day when I caught my first sight of the high walls around Taiyuan, which was to be my missionary post for several years. I knew that it was here, outside the huge city gate, that they had thrown the bodies of the Protestant and Catholic missionaries who had been massacred by the Boxers six years before my arrival." [12]

The Taiyuan massacre took place on July 9, 1900, when Shanxi Governor Yu-Hsien, having taken the precaution to have the gates of the city closed and carefully watched, commanded all the foreigners, including 50 Protestant and Catholic missionaries in the city, to appear before him, sending armed soldiers to enforce his orders.

Yu-Hsien enjoined them to prostrate at his feet, accusing them of bringing vice, evil, and unhappiness to the Central Kingdom. There was only one remedy for such evil, and that was to behead them all. The order was to be carried out in Yu-Hsien's presence.

Two Roman Catholic Bishops and three other missionaries were then led out, and were the first to be decapitated on the spot. Then one and all – men, women, and children – were mercilessly beheaded in the courtyard in front of the hall in which they had been received in audience, and well in sight of Yu-Hsien.

Insult – no greater could be given in China – was added to injury by taking the bodies outside the city walls and leaving them to the dogs instead of burying them. The rebellion continued for some time in Taiyuan, with two hundred Chinese Christians being put to death five days later, so that by the end of August a total of 159 Protestant and Catholics, including 46 children, had been murdered in Shanxi province. [13]

Albert wondered how enduring would be the "Boxer Protocol", the Peace Agreement signed in 1900 between the Qing Imperial Court and the Eight-Nation Alliance. The Agreement had resulted in the execution of Yu-Hsien and appointment of a successor who supported the return of Christian missionaries, and included using some of the repatriation money paid by the Chinese Government to establish a university for Chinese students. Albert was not yet to know, but the initiative would directly affect his career pathway through the 30 years he spent in China.

On Sunday morning the new, freshly attired missionary went to a church service in the city's cathedral wearing his best London suit.

Taiyuan Cathedral 1907 – Source: Wikipedia.

A surprise awaited him. "I saw that the interior of the church was divided by a curtain of blue material, about six feet high. The part facing the pulpit was for men, while the other section was for women, who could hear the voice of the preacher but who could only see him by standing on their benches." [14]

Even though Albert did not understand the language, he retained a vivid memory of his first Chinese service – "Everything seemed so strange: the singing of the hymns, especially the Chinese melodies whose scale consists of only five tones; the Bible reading; the sermon delivered by a Chinese preacher who kept his hat on all the time."

After the service, one question filled his heart with fear: "Will I ever manage to preach in Chinese?" As Albert hadn't time to acquire Chinese clothes, his suit included a black silk top-hat worn at the time by nearly all English clergymen. His missionary colleague informed him after the service that one of the deacons had said to him: "The new missionary wears a very fine hat; but why not advise him to add a nice big red silk pompom on top of it?" Was this an insult, a joke or a serious recommendation? Albert never knew, but he quickly began to learn that his new compatriots had a philosophic sense of humour.

7

He was grateful for the opportunity to live in China for a few years before the great upheaval which resulted in China becoming a republic in 1912. Between 1906 and 1911, he got to know inland China under the Qing dynasty; "Old China", a time when a multitude of ancient customs could sometimes make life very complicated, especially for a newcomer. Yet the lifestyle was basically simple, almost patriarchal but open and honest, where people had no need to lock their doors, even during the night.

Two of Albert's most striking early impressions were of seeing men wear their hair in long pigtails and women wearing incredibly small shoes. The men's pigtails amused him: "I could easily imagine what would have happened to them in a fight between schoolboys in my country!" Later, he came to realise that the Chinese can find poetic inspiration even in a man's pigtail. The following is a rough translation from one of China's greatest poets: "With my white hair could be plaited a long, long rope, which still would not reach the depth of my woes."

As for the women's tiny feet, which prevented them from walking properly, Albert recalled the description given by one of his colleagues one day when, during a trip into the countryside, they had seen an elderly woman cross the yard. "'Look at her,' said my companion, 'she looks like a goat who's being forced to walk on its hind legs!' But then again, what about the tiny pinched-in waists of European ladies at that time?"

Both customs – pigtails and women's tight shoes – had dynastic 'political' control elements and would soon be removed.

One of Albert's greatest difficulties in the beginning was to know how to conduct himself towards others as a man of standing. This was something which at the time was considered in China to be of great importance. A new missionary was required to study a book of rules, known as "the compass", to guide his path, but which Albert found difficult to understand.

"Sometimes I thought I would make fewer mistakes if I simply did the opposite of what I would normally do!" For a long while, Albert could not get used to the indirect nature of everyday language. If, for example, a master wanted to dismiss a servant who had become useless, he would not say "I no longer need you. You can go". Instead, he would say: "Don't you think your father needs you back at home?" or something similar.

Difficulties arose in day-to-day relationships. One day, a young lad working for the mission caught a bad cold. Albert advised him: "Go and spend a couple of days at home, it will do you good." To his amazement, the youth burst into tears and said: "What have I done? Why do you want to get rid of me? Have I failed in my duty?" Little wonder, then that the Chinese are such expert diplomats!

In learning Chinese, Albert noticed something similar: that a "Yes" in Chinese could approximate to "No" in French; that if a Chinese person wanted to say that one village was near another, he would say, "It isn't far," and if it was a long way, he would say that it "wasn't near"; if he wanted to say that a particular man was a fine fellow, he would say: "So and so is not too bad."

Truth is that which "is not false". A *lie* is that which "is not true". If a church-member wanted to say that the sermon had been too long, he would politely say that the preacher had "not been brief" – and so it went on. You have to get used to this Chinese way of thinking and expression, and you begin to do so in language study.

It was similar with respect to daily customs. Albert recalled a holiday festival for the Chinese New Year: The clothes worn by a child were often identical to those worn by his father. The child wore a little round hat, just like his father's, with a red bobble on top, a short black silk coat with very long sleeves, an ankle-length robe, white stockings and black shoes.

On another occasion, he came across a funeral. The coffin, carried by eight men, was surrounded by a crowd of unkempt, ragged beggars. "I was told they were there to receive alms from the deceased person. In the funeral procession were five or six gentlemen, obviously the closest relatives, dressed in long white robes, who were weeping very loudly, while behind them a crowd of neighbours and friends followed making heart-rending lamentations. I was struck, obviously, by the use of white instead of black as the colour of mourning."

Another memory is that of a professional beggar whom Albert saw sitting near the city gates with his little bowl on the ground in front of him waiting for alms from the passers-by. "I said to my companion 'professional beggar', since this is what he was, just like those in Europe during the Middle-Ages that Victor Hugo described, and that are in the writings of Erasmus which have been preserved with such skill by Charles Reade in *The Cloister and the Hearth*.

"The difference is that those belonged to the Europe of the Middle Ages while mine belonged to 19th century China." But Albert's companion responded: "You would think he was a beggar, but in fact he owns a fine house in the city. He knows me and when I go past, he gives me a knowing smile, as if to say: 'We share a secret.'"

Albert was scandalised by this and said so, but his colleague simply smiled and said: "You'll see plenty of others if you stay here long enough." Albert wanted to check it for himself, so one evening he followed 'the beggar' and sure enough he entered the yard of a fine house. "I stood watching from a corner and later that evening, I saw him come out, dressed in fine clothes, to take his evening walk."

Albert soon experienced first-hand examples of Chinese 'face-saving' cultural practice or what he called a Chinese true generosity of spirit. A missionary colleague told him of an experience during an official meeting, when he had unintentionally broken one of the rules of etiquette. Immediately, the leading mandarin, in front of everybody, made the same gaffe. It was his way of 'saving face' for his colleague.

"Subsequently, the practice came back to me one evening when I had the opportunity to imitate that mandarin. I was one of twelve people invited to a small dinner given by the wife of one of our missionaries in honour of the local mandarin. Unfortunately, one of the dishes was a plum pie. Etiquette required that the most important guest, in this case the mandarin, should be the first to taste the pie.

"I immediately realised his predicament as he put the first plum into his mouth. What should he do with the stone? Unable to swallow it, he did what he would have done at home, namely he spat it out into a corner of the dining room! It was then that I remembered the great mandarin who had saved my colleague's face, and I loudly spat my first plum stone to the opposite corner of the room. There followed a hailstorm of plum stones which had to be swept up the following morning!"[15]

Once Albert began to speak Chinese well enough to be able to get by on his own, he shifted into a small two-roomed house near the southern gates of the city.

The memory of his first house continued to hold a large place in his life, for two particular reasons: the first is that it was where he first met Jessie, the woman who was to become his "brave and faithful companion for more than fifty years".[16] The other reason is that during his stay in this house, "I was able to get to know the Chinese people better than if I had lived in the European community".

One of his early concerns was to manage the finances of the house and day-to-day living. For Europeans living in the Chinese hinterland a Chinese servant was required, a 'boy' who was responsible for all the details of daily life. "In terms of age, my 'boy' could have been my father, my colleagues having advised me to choose someone of mature years. His name was 'Lao Ta', which means 'the elder'; a fine man, but without any concept of the life and habits of a European. But he was exactly what I needed."

Another matter Albert had to get used to was the Chinese currency. "I made my first visit to a bank in Taiyuan, to find myself in a small plain room, overlooking a little courtyard, with a single employee sitting at his table with his writing brush and abacus in front of him." Albert was given a bank book, a sort of little accordion measuring two inches long by four inches high, squeezed into a holder on which the clerk wrote his Chinese name: 'Chia Li Yen'.

"What about the cheque book?" I asked. He looked amazed, but smiled and said: "No need for cheques. As long as you're in credit, you can withdraw from here any money that you need by presenting this book." Albert walked out of the bank astonished by this simplicity, especially since he had been told that the banks in Shanxi were famous throughout China.

The most common Chinese currency was made of brass, in coins a little smaller than a French 'sou', with a square hole through the middle to enable you to thread them on a string and tie together about a hundred coins to make a commercially viable unit known as a 'ligature'. Since each coin carried an indication of the period when it was minted, he tried to decipher the date of some of the coins which Lao Ta used to buy vegetables and eggs, and was totally amazed to discover that in 1908 he was using coins which dated from the 11th century! [17]

There was one difficulty with the house which gave Albert real problems; every evening, an army of rats from outside climbed the badly constructed walls and invaded the ceiling, fighting and scrabbling very noisily above his head! "There was no point getting a cat, since the rats would have eaten it! But on a visit to Peking, I got hold of a cross bow with clay bolts. Lying in bed, I fired at random towards the rats in the ceiling and I managed to kill one. I am not sure why, but from then onwards, there was a marked reduction in the noise of their fighting."

During this period, he learnt much about the Chinese people that was useful to him later. In particular, he discovered the importance of the Chinese family and the authority of its head: the father. For as long as he lived, the father was the acknowledged head, which was not without its problems, especially for the children who were beginning to receive a modern education. "As an example of the authority of the Chinese father: during a session of the Church Council, we were considering an application from a man in his sixties who wanted to become a member of the Taiyuan church. We were surprised to hear him say that he still had some 'idols' at home. The chairman said: 'But since you've told us you no longer believe in them, why haven't you got rid of them?' The reply was immediate: 'My father won't allow it.' And yet the speaker was himself the grey-haired father of a large family."

The importance of the father was also reflected in the distinction made in China between boys and girls. A son was a gift from heaven, while a daughter was just the opposite.

In the wall surrounding the courtyard of a Roman Catholic convent, there was a small opening from which projected a basin made of cement; it was there to receive the after-birth of little girls whose parents did not want them. "Rather see that," Albert said to himself, "than to see the small bodies barely covered with a tattered rag, thrown off the town wall and eaten by dogs," which he had seen with grief and horror on several occasions.

"However, I would not want to give a false impression. Living close to me, there was an elderly Chinese man who often took a walk in the evening with a small girl in his arms, showing her the caged birds." But it was a fact that in China at that time, a boy represented the hope of the family, while a girl was a problem to be resolved one way or another, as early as possible. It made Albert question the completeness of the Chinese ideal that they were a civilized society.

During his early years in Taiyuan, another thing he never managed to understand was the almost total separation between the sexes in public, even in church services. "I knew Mr Kao, for example, one of the elders of the church, but nobody would have dreamt of introducing me to Mrs Kao. At an early stage I had been warned by the Dean of the Mission that if I happened to meet a missionary lady in the street, it would have been quite inappropriate to raise my hat to her, or even to show that I had noticed her.

"What you would not be able to imagine without having witnessed it is the painful way these poor women walked with their artificially deformed feet." In literary Chinese, a woman's foot is called 'Ching Lien', which means 'Golden Lily', after an expression used by a sixth century poet. "I would have liked to tell that poet a thing or two," said Albert. "The torture began when a Chinese girl reached the age of about five." He was told that one in ten girls died as a result.

It was not until after the 1911 Revolution that foot binding was phased out and the education of girls began in the whole of China.

Early on, Albert gained a view of the way China was divided into social classes. This was summed up in four words which even Lao Ta knew by heart although he probably could not read them: 'Shih', 'Nung', 'Kung', 'Shang'.

The nation was generally divided between the Emperor and the People. The former was regarded as appointed by the will of Heaven and as the parent of the latter. Besides being emperor, he was also law-giver, commander-in-chief of the armies, high priest, and master of ceremonies.

The people were divided into four classes: (1) 'Shih', Officers (later Scholars), consisting of Ch'en, Officials (a few of whom are enabled), and Shen Shih, Gentry; (2) 'Nung', Agriculturalists, the cultivators of the soil; (3) 'Kung', Artisans, later including workers and/or producers; (4) 'Shang', Merchants, who produce nothing, but work for themselves.[18]

This is a very ancient tradition and it is possible that the merchants were not always the least respected members of Chinese society. As Albert travelled out to China, he had noticed that in the great sea ports, long before he reached China, the shops seemed to be largely, if not almost entirely, in the hands of the Chinese. "Far from being the last, they appeared to be certainly the most prosperous." As for the soldiers, they were outside the class system! Albert questioned: "Can you make a man out of a soldier?"

He also found out early on how important in the thinking and life of the Chinese people was the belief in an invisible world, filled with spirits. "You may dismiss it as folklore. But it is a plant whose roots reach every part of Chinese life. Its influence is to be found in the great affairs of life, but also in the smallest details, including the name to be given to a boy or the clothes his mother will make for him as a child."

You might think that this general belief in an invisible world would make the task of a Christian missionary that much easier. "Yes and no," said Albert. "Yes, for the soil was in a sense already prepared; but no, because it was already teeming with a dense covering of vegetation which threatened to choke any new seed."

At the same time, most Chinese people had great tolerance and curiosity in religious matters. "From my earliest days in China, I met people who simply could not understand why, in the Christian religion, there are so many denominations, often at odds with each other; and why the Bible Society has to publish two different editions of the Bible, in one of which the name of 'God' is translated as 'Shen' (Spirit) and in the other by 'Shangti' (the Sovereign from on High), without mentioning the Catholics, who use the term 'Tien Chu' (Lord of Heaven)."

Albert found it difficult to untangle the religious conditions. The three great religious systems – Confucianism, Buddhism and Taoism – were still influencing the people as they had done for hundreds of years. But it would be a mistake to regard Chinese people giving allegiance to one or other of these systems. The Chinese saying 'San chiao wei I' – the three religions are one – means that a Chinese may belong, in a sense, to all three at one and the same time. Confucianism had, in practice, lost sight of the deeply religious basis on which the ancient religion of China stood. It had become mainly a system of behaviour, regulating right relationships between a man and his fellows. Buddhism and Taoism, in the mind of the ordinary person, had become hopelessly mixed in the practice of everyday life.[19]

It is different in the case of Mohammedanism and Christianity, Albert noted. 'A Mohammedan is a Mohammedan and a Christian is a Christian.' However, he was well aware that within Christianity, a 'Protestant' is not a 'Catholic' – they had been at war with each other in the Waldensian valleys for centuries.

Although China in 1949 declared itself to be an atheist society, both Protestantism and Catholicism were added to the officially recognised Chinese religious systems of Buddhism, Taoism and Islam. Early 21st century estimates are that some 80% of China's population, which is around 1.5 billion people, practice some kind of Chinese folk religion, 15% are Buddhists, 10% Taoist, 2% Protestant, 0.8% Muslim and 0.3% Catholic.[20]

The state of education in Taiyuan was far from ideal. The vast majority of the population remained illiterate, while the few who were educated kept a closed mind to the scientific discoveries which were bringing a big change in the life of the West. But one of the deepest impressions on Albert's work in Baptist Missionary Schools in Shanxi (and later Shantung) was the eagerness of Chinese boys to go to school.[21] "I was amazed to see each year small boys coming to us from distant villages to sit for the entrance examination to the central school in the station. To suspend a boy from attending classes, even only for a short time, would have been for him the worst form of punishment."

Albert – dressed to teach.

Later on, when Albert worked in Shanghai with a team of Chinese who had studied in Europe or the United States, he was asked to give a talk about his life as a missionary in Shanxi and Shantung. After his talk, a Chinese woman came up to him and said: "You told me so much about my country which I didn't know myself. I always lived in one of the large cities before going abroad for a few years. What you've said has made me feel really nostalgic for my country."

Another early memory that Albert said he would prefer to forget, centred on the mission's hospital and a soldier patient. "In order to practice my Chinese as much as possible, I went to chat to the patients. One day, when I was there, some soldiers from the local garrison brought in one of their number, laid out on a stretcher and covered in a coarse sheet. When the doctor lifted the sheet, we were appalled: the poor boy's thighs were reduced to pulp over an area the size of a plate. He had been beaten for having failed one of his duties. I wanted to say something, but my Chinese was not up to the task. For his part, the doctor who was a veteran, in a few eloquent words spelt out the consequences of this barbaric punishment and made no secret of his fear that this poor soldier's life was in danger. And sure enough, he died in hospital a few days later."

Chapter 2:   THE 1911 REVOLUTION

IN Taiyuan, Albert was to experience a 'revolution', an event which began a deep change in the very structure of Chinese society and lifestyle and still continues today.

The Revolution of 1911 ended 2000 years of imperial rule and 276 years of the Manchu-led Qing Dynasty, and led to the establishment of the Republic of China, with an elected President, and a Parliament consisting of a Senate and House of Representatives. The various government departments were reorganized on Western lines, and a large number of new offices instituted.

There was little doubt, Albert wrote in 1945, that the Boxer rebels in 1900 were acting with the knowledge and approval of the Manchu Empress, Tzu Hsi, when hundreds of foreigners and thousands of Chinese Christians were murdered.[22]

Following the Boxer Rising, it was clear to all reformers that China would never take its proper place among modern nations as long as the Manchu monarchy remained in power. It was only three years after the death of Tzu Hsi that the 1911 Revolution broke out.

The actual outbreak on October 10th, 1911 came as a surprise to most people, and yet the Revolutionary Party had been preparing for some time. Plans had been laid in advance, and the line of action to be followed in each provincial capital city settled beforehand.

This was one of the reasons why this greatest of all Chinese revolutions was accomplished, comparatively speaking, with little bloodshed, Albert claimed. In Taiyuan, for example, Albert was kept informed from time to time of coming events by one of the Chinese Christians, who told the mission when to collect together all the foreigners in one place in the city.

Prewarned that the arrival of soldiers of the Republic was imminent, the 20 missionaries, including small children, who happened to be in the city from across the province for their annual conference, were gathered to the same place, close to the hospital.

Shooting started about 6.30am on Sunday, 29th October, directed at two main points: the Manchu Garrison – killing most of the soldiers – and the city-centre where the government offices and residences of the highest officials of the province were situated. "It was at this point that I first saw and heard those who were running away, as the Manchu garrison was close to the hospital."

"How could I ever forget those crowds of men, women and small children whom I saw taking flight in panic pursued by gunfire? How could I ever forget the cries of distress I heard from every side?"

Shooting continued throughout the morning and a small canon was hoisted onto the city wall. "You can imagine my surprise at the arrival out of breath of Lao Ta, my man-servant, with a jug full of milk for my daughter, Enrica, aged two months. 'Weren't you frightened?' I asked him. 'Yes,' he replied, adding with typical Chinese fatalism, 'I was afraid for my pitcher'."

In the afternoon the gunfire stopped; the revolution seemed to be over and the revolutionaries could have a rest. But it was not the end. That night one of Albert's colleagues woke him. "Come quickly," he said, "and see what's going on." The sky above their heads was red, and the city centre was on fire. All along the main streets, flames reached up to the sky. "A deafening clamour rose up, but it was no longer the cries of despair of the poor souls pursued by the gunfire. It was the savage cries of the riffraff who were in control for the moment and were looting the shops and banks."

Albert couldn't find out exactly what had happened, but soon had proof that the chief of the revolutionary party, General Xishan, had no intention of letting the hooligans ruin the cause of the new Republic! Indeed, in spite of the rather alarming rumours circulating, order was soon restored, so much so that within two days it was possible for Albert to go on a tour of inspection to find out what had happened.

He was surprised to meet on one of the main streets hundreds of students from the university, arranged in companies, armed with rifles and bayonets, and in brand new uniforms – "an indication, surely, of the preparation that had been made beforehand."

The Manchu Court, unable to fight, and unwilling to spend its financial resources, ceased all opposition.

On his tour, Albert saw at once that the looters had been severely punished. Those whom the soldiers had succeeded in catching had been executed on the spot. Stuck on the forehead of each was a small piece of red paper with a few words to indicate their crime, and the heads were hung by their long pigtails on the nearest telegraph pole. "For a long time, the memory of those heads hung along the main thoroughfare of the city kept me awake at nights."

Other looters who had taken flight with their booty had been pursued by the soldiers, cut down and executed like the others. "I saw down the side streets where I ventured, several bodies each with a little heap of stolen goods beside it.

"In the courtyards of the Imperial Government, I saw the bodies of several officials who had been shot by the Republicans. The body of the governor was there, and that of his sons, one of whom was in military uniform. They were still lying there awaiting burial."

"The days that followed were not easy for our little band of missionaries. The Republicans in Taiyuan had won the day, but what was happening in Peking (Beijing), with (Army general) Yuan Shikai, who seemed to lean first to the Imperial party and then towards the new Republic?"[23] It was at this point that the mission received a message from Sir John Jordan, British Minister in China, who advised all those who could, to leave the interior of China, at least for the time being.

"For us missionaries there was never any question of abandoning our churches, but on the other hand the presence of a number of families could be an embarrassment, if not an actual danger, for everyone, including the Chinese Christians. So, the task of remaining with our Chinese brethren was entrusted to three of our oldest missionaries with one of our young doctors, whilst the others followed the advice of the minister."

But there remained the problem of how they were to leave Taiyuan. "Luckily, we had a friend among those in authority in the new regime. We had at our disposal a railway-carriage due to leave a few days later. It was thus that we reached Peking one Sunday evening, greeted enthusiastically by the missionaries of the capital who saw us as 'refugees' from the revolution in Taiyuan."

On 2nd January, Albert, his wife Jessie and their daughter, Enrica, aged 4-months, left for Europe by the trans-Siberian railway – a journey via Harbin, Irkutsk, Moscow, Warsaw, Berlin, Holland, and England, all in mid-winter, before World War I. They had to cross Moscow from one station to another in a drosky.[24]

Years later, after World War II and the atomic bombing of Hiroshima, Albert was convinced that the 1911 Revolution was one of the most far-reaching events, not only in the history of China, but the history of the world. In 1945, Albert agreed with French historian, Henri Cordier, who noted that there are many topics of interest in Europe and America, but there is not one which is as important for the future of the world as the 1911 Revolution.

For Albert, the Revolution involved a change in the Chinese people themselves. "It has come out of a re-examination of values, a re-orientation of life which may bring with it the repudiation of an ancient tradition." [25] The idea of China as a giant asleep for centuries, now waking out of sleep, is not an accurate description of what is happening, he wrote. "China is not like an old man, suddenly awakened. She is like a young giant refreshed."

While China has had a long past, Albert saw China in 1911 as essentially a nation of young people, full of the ardour, enthusiasm, hope and also the inexperience of youth.

The overthrow of the Manchu Dynasty and establishment of the Republic of China in 1911 was soon to involve Albert directly in helping to introduce reforms which played a part in the great awakening of China.

Chapter 3:   FROM PREACHER TO TEACHER

ALBERT returned to China in early 1913, spiritually refreshed by an emotional visit to Torre Pellice. He was keenly looking forward to resuming the teaching role he had been assigned just before the 1911 Revolution.

Albert's parents had both been teachers, and he strongly believed that all young people (male and female equally) should have access to as much education as they are intellectually capable of receiving. Consistent with the Waldensian belief system, the curriculum should be as wide as possible – mathematics, science, biology, literature and languages – to enable all students to make their own way to discovering the love of God through awareness of all beauties and gifts with which the Lord has endowed the world.

The visit to Val Pellice had reinforced Albert's calling to become a missionary. "It was good to wander again among those snow-clad hills, and among those valleys, where caves have been used as churches, and where every mountain stream has flowed red with the blood of men and women who esteemed it a gain to die rather than to deny their Lord, and to follow the trail over the passes so rich in memory for the Israel of the Alps: 'For the strength of the Hills we bless Thee, Our God, our Fathers' God.'"

As he walked up the valleys, "somehow I knew I belonged to the place," he wrote later when back in China. A raw wildness clothed the valleys where even wild deer could still be seen. He was home, and visited with Jessie the nearby cavern-church near the head of the Angrogna Valley, where you must crawl to enter. Used by persecuted groups centuries ago, it has a hidden look-out window commanding the valley-approach.

Albert also took the opportunity to attend the Waldensian Synod held every year in the autumn, and in particular the reception of delegates from foreign Churches especially the Moderators of the Presbyterian churches of England and Scotland. "Well do I remember listening with wonder at the noble efforts of some of these delegates to speak a word of greeting in Italian, with inevitable quotations from Dante or Petrarch, and to watch the solemn face of the long-bearded chairman, as he thought of the words of welcome that he would have to address to each of the delegates."

Reinforcing Albert's deeply held Waldensian beliefs, he recalled that the most unique experience that occurred on this Torre Pellice visit, was the conducting of an English service for a British congregation in one of the old Waldensian churches build in 1555. "At the foot of each pillar in the church lies a member of an English or Scottish nobleman's family, sites chosen because they preferred to be buried in Waldensian ground. On each of the pillars there is a marble tablet with a Latin inscription, and I remember how as a school boy I used to practice my Latin on those inscriptions instead of listening to the sermon."

Earlier during the trip back to Europe from China, Albert met Jessie's family in Blackheath, London, for the first time. Then Jessie was taken to meet Albert's family in Torre Pellice, before they (with daughter Enrica) returned to Taiyuan, via Moscow and across Siberia, arriving in time for Walter's birth in March 2013.

Albert had been put in charge of the newly opened Taiyuan Boys High School – established from repatriation funds paid by the Chinese Government to the countries whose missionaries, including the whole of the Shanxi staff, had been massacred in the Boxer Rising in 1900. By now Albert was an expert linguist in Chinese, speaking with perfect ease and accuracy and which was readily understood by all the Chinese present.

The appointment came about at the suggestion of Dr Timothy Richard, a senior missionary who had helped the Qing government to deal with the aftermath of the Taiyuan massacre during the Boxer Rebellion. Dr Richard recommended that younger missionaries like 'Garnier' spend some hours each week teaching English to the University students. He thought the main cause of China's social problems was lack of education of the population, so he proposed to the Qing court the establishment of a modern university in Taiyuan with Boxer indemnity money paid to Great Britain.

Both proposals were agreed – Albert added education (teaching English) to his activities, and Taiyuan gained a university, one of the three earliest modern universities in China and still going strong.[26] Dr Richard was in charge of the fund to build Taiyuan University until 1912, and went on to establish the Christian Literature Society in Shanghai which Albert was later to head (1926).

Albert enjoyed teaching. In 1915 he sought and was appointed the first head master of the Gotch Robinson High School for Boys in Tsingchow, Shantung Province.

Albert (seated, crossed legs, right mid-section) inaugural principal of Gotch Robinson High School for Boys in Tsingchow, Shantung Province – around 1920.

Also, although far from the scene of World War I, Albert longed to help. He wanted to be involved in the war directly. His brother, Emile, was fighting with the Italian Alpine troops in his capacity as an engineer. The only way Albert could think of helping the war effort in the early stages was to auction his stamp collection which he had begun almost as soon as stamps came into use.

One of the stamps had an inverted centre. Many years later, in Shanghai, he happened to meet the auctioneer who reminded him of this stamp, by then of fabulous worth. The collection went for $1,000 – a year's salary in those days. Albert was given a medal at the end of the war in recognition of the fact that his was the highest donation to the Italian Red Cross from any individual.

Another opportunity for Albert to contribute to the war arose when Chinese coolies were being recruited for work behind the lines in France. Men were needed in China who could help the War Office to arrange for the embarkation of these men, and then for their well-being and work in France. Several of the Baptist missionaries in Shantung, where this work with the coolies took place, resigned temporarily for six months from the mission and were employed by the War Office for that period.

Albert was also prepared to go to France with the coolie-drafts, where his tri-lingual ability would have been useful, but the complication of his Italian nationality was seen as an obstacle. Instead, Albert worked on administration tasks at Waihaiwei, the chief point of embarkation for those going to France, and he was there when my (real) father, Ben, was born in April, 1917.

Meanwhile establishing the Gotch Robinson High School proved a difficult mission. Power in Tsingchow, and across Shuntung Province, was increasingly in the hands of war-lords and soldiers turned bandits in lieu of the pay they failed to receive. "The common people suffered terribly, from government officials on the one hand and from bandits on the other. Shantung was one of the worst affected areas in China," Albert recalled. "Outlaws hid in the crops, and attacked anyone who seemed to have any money in his pocket or at home. There is no security for the peaceful traveler or merchant."

In Shantung when an express train was stopped by bandits, they took all the passengers away to their hideouts in the hills and held them there to ransom for several weeks. Among them were several influential foreigners, including United States businessman John Rockefeller's sister-in-law. "While this event received great publicity simply because many foreigners were among the captives, but the fact was that there were hundreds of Chinese prisoners already on those hills – old men, women and children, who have been there for months: Who cares about them?"

A little boy was kidnapped and the bandits demanded a certain sum for his ransom. The parents, after selling all they had, could only raise half the sum which they forwarded to the bandits. "The wretches sent back half the child."

A few days after the bandit scare began, Albert had to travel to the nearby province of Honan, to an interprovincial church council meeting. "You can imagine how I disliked the prospect of leaving my wife and little Ben alone! My wife never said a word, although Ben told me afterwards when I got back, that she cried a good deal after I had gone." [27]

The pastor of one of the parishes only a few miles from the city, had a terrible experience in the village where he resided. Having collected information on where the richest family of the village lived, the bandits went to the pastor, and pointing a pistol at his head, ordered him to lead the way to the house. "The poor man took them along. When they got there, the outside gate was barred, of course, because in times like these, people are particularly careful, and will not open the door unless they recognize the voice of the people who call. The bandits got on both sides of the poor pastor, and pointing a pistol on each side of his head, they quietly ordered him to call to the people inside to open the door. What could the wretched man do? He called, and the unsuspecting folk

23

opened the door, whereupon the bandits rushed in and took the eldest boy of the family."

Albert pleaded with London: "Please don't be too hard on the pastor. There is no law out here, whatever folk may write or say in public speeches. The people living in the country are entirely at the mercy of these lawless bands. They dare not even defend themselves against the bandits who have their spies everywhere. And if they decide to speak against the established authority which should protect them, it is even worse."

While visiting Shantung village churches alone, Albert dropped into what was none other than a nest of bandits. He did not realise it till he had departed, but greeted and chatted with them and eventually left without tremor or fear. Then it came over him in a flash the danger he had passed through. If he had behaved differently, he would almost certainly have lost his life. "I caught in retrospect the smiles which showed that the bandits thought me only a harmless foreign fool."

In 1924, Albert was invited to join the Christian Literature Society (CLS) in Shanghai. The school committee, however, decided that he could not be spared and wanted him to carry on with the proposed development of the school. Although Albert felt drawn to transfer to Shanghai, he deferred to the school's wishes, observing that in the case of the mission's educational works, "We can educate our boys best by leading them to know a few things well and by giving them a healthy appetite for learning more, rather than by chasing them through all manner of subjects with ornamental names, and leaving them in the end so poverty-stricken as to believe that the world has no further mysteries for them."

By 1925, there were riots in many places, and a strong anti-foreign feeling. Great Britain was labelled as the enemy of mankind, and blamed for all the troubles in China. The missionary's Chinese pastors were singled out, one being attacked in the main street of the town for having helped a missionary to light his kitchen fire.

A turning point came when the Shanghai shootings gave rise to anti-foreign boycotts and mob violence, in which student protest played a leading part. The time had come! The danger from bandits in Shantung was increasing in severity. Many Chinese children had been cruelly abducted for ransom. Might not foreign children also be subjected to this? Also, his three children, Enrica now 13, Walter and Ben, 11 and 8, needed to continue their education. So, it was clear that they should return to England. Should their mother accompany them, or could a suitable escort be found to travel with the children? It was decided that Albert remain in China alone, so in June 1925 he escorted the family from the Shantung port of Tsingtuo to Shanghai and onto a ship to Tilbury, England. A family separation began which continued until 1937.

Albert's work continued, but conditions worsened. "All manner of false accusations were levelled against us, and even, I am sorry to say, a Christian was heard loudly to advocate the policy of 'kill these foreign devils'. This man owes all he has directly to Baptist Mission Society missionaries. Some of our friends did not desert us, however. Help we could not get, because it could not have been offered in secret, but there was no lack of provisions. Mysterious hens began to lay eggs in the school grounds, and even some ducks seemed to trespass in like manner, while a new species of apricot began to grow among turnips.

"Even parcels of meat seemed to appear in unforeseen places, while it was easy to understand from the faces of many that had they not dreaded the vengeance of those terrible schoolboys – 'the hope of China' – they would have come openly to the rescue. Not one of the missionaries suffered unduly."

But a drought meant the price of food went up so rapidly that the school had to close a few days earlier than planned. A letter from Albert to London gave assurance that despite the commercial, racial and other problems that filled the minds of both Chinese and foreigners, Christians and non-Christians alike, "We are not forgetting what our task is".

"I think, however, that the worst feature in the situation is that one hears no cry of indignation against these shameful deeds. You hear of students storming against imperialist Britain, the oppressor of the weak, and yet not a voice is raised against the daily oppression of their own folk."

In spite of all the difficulties the school had repeated successes in exams. "I was able to remain at my post, without showing resentment against the really vile accusations that were levelled against us. The local Chinese pastor, Mr. Feng and I grew in mutual affection and esteem."

The Tsingchow school sent more boys to the Shantung Christian University than any other school in China. They took first place, both in actual numbers of boys who went forward and also the percentage of passes at the entrance examination, and kept that place for a number of years. "It was not easy to win or keep that place."

Throughout Albert's tenure until 1926, the growing weakness of the Republican Government fueled civil disturbances and incidents of banditry which made life almost intolerable, particularly in the countryside.

Meanwhile back in Shanghai the Christian Literature Society continued to seek Albert's services. With education in Shantung becoming nearly impossible on account of the drought and anti-foreign feeling stirred up by Bolshevik influence and the effect this had on students, staff and himself, the decision to move to Shanghai was taken, and Albert transferred in 1926.

Albert returned to Tsingchow for a visit in 1933. The school had closed in 1929 amid the changes in the education system after the Nationalists took over Shandong province and withdrawing the mission was under consideration.

For Albert there was another matter for even greater concern – "the religious revival which is spreading in various parts of Shantung." Much of it seemed genuine and was accompanied by a new desire for Bible study. "But the movement has its dangers," Albert wrote in a letter. "Our pastors are worried as to what they should do. How can they conserve the true elements of the movement, and how can they help the people avoid giving themselves to artificial emotional performances which have no bearing on daily life?"

The church in Shantung was passing through a critical stage. Albert summed up: "Never before has the need of sound knowledge of the Bible been more manifest. Banditry, misgovernment, famine and epidemics, have reduced village life to a nightmare in many districts. The minds of the people are taut, and their hearts are heavy. Is not this the opportunity for the Church of Christ?"

Chapter 4: CALLED TO SHANGHAI

ARRIVING at the Christian Literature Society office in Shanghai in September 1926, Albert was welcomed enthusiastically and plunged into action on a long list of tough assignments.

All Christian organisations were facing great difficulties at this time but the general feeling was one of hope. The Society, representing all denominations except Catholics, shared this outlook. But Albert was aware that the Society was not quite ready to take advantage of the new opportunities. New blood was wanted in the organisation, more Chinese staff needed to be recruited, more original writing was required, and finally they needed new premises. The Society's building location was inconvenient and too small. Albert was among those who believed that progress was imperative and possible, and led with enthusiasm the many tasks that lay ahead.

Albert spent 10 years in Shanghai, the last seven as General Secretary of the Society, and the last European to hold this post. Albert lamented the lack of Chinese leadership, but realized that the time was not yet ripe for a general handover of responsibility.

In the 10 years since the retirement of Dr Timothy Richard, General Secretary from 1891-1916, and the impact of World War I, the activity and influence of the Society had fallen away. When Dr Richard reached China in 1869 the life of the country was at its lowest ebb – a dreary formalism had produced a period of stagnation. The Imperial Court was degenerate, good officials few and far between, and all relations with the outside world unwelcome. China's past seemed to be blocking the way to the future.

Believing, like Albert, that Christianity was "good news for the whole man," Dr Richard worked out his belief in his own way: He persistently tried to reach and influence the scholar class whose ignorance both of the physical world and the course of history blocked all progress. Dr Richard's character and his appreciation of the good in China's civilisation won him great respect, and many high officials profited by his advice and good sense. He emphasised from the beginning the importance of sound education along modern lines. When Dr Richard became General Secretary, he set himself to produce a notable series of books and periodicals which had a deep influence on the future of China.

In *A Maker of Modern China,* Albert notes the meticulous work Dr Richard undertook to show Chinese officials the folly of a reactionary policy on the part of the Chinese Government. As a preparation for meetings in Nanking,

Wuchang and Beijing and elsewhere he had drawn up the outline of a 12-year programme "for the material, social, intellectual and spiritual welfare of China", making it clear that, according to him, the spiritual development came first, for without it, "there could be no stability in any other department". Dr Richard took 500 copies of this programme to be distributed with care.[28]

The Society's work was to be done for the whole of China, for all denominations, as well as for non-Christian seekers after truth. A five-strong leadership group indicates the nature and scope of the work undertaken: There was Alexander Williamson, the founder, a Scotsman and Presbyterian; Ernst Faber, a German and Lutheran; Dr Timothy Richard, a Welshman and a Baptist; and Ts'ai Erh K'ang, a Chinese and a Confucian scholar.[29]

The group believed that the chief source of China's disasters in her relationships with the West was to be found in its ignorance of how a positive relationship could be established. "The rising anti-foreign feeling, with its fatal consequences for missionary work, was a direct result of this ignorance." Dr Richard proposed a two-pronged programme – first, a campaign to reach Chinese leaders by periodicals, books, pamphlets and presentations showing the progress of Western enlightenment in regard to material, social and political welfare of the people; and, second, by showing the supreme power of the moral and spiritual truths of Christianity to bring about general reformation. "Both are needed", and "funds contributed will be applied to either or both according to the wishes of the subscribers."

A series of academic publications appealing to Chinese scholars showed how the East and the West could help each other. "Suffice to say," concluded Albert, "that by universal consent, these books were among the most effective means in bringing about, and in directing, the Chinese movement towards reform, as well pointed out in a leading article of *The Times*."

When Albert became General Secretary in 1929, he set about refreshing the Society's publication efforts to introduce popular books readable over the whole of China, some of them obligatory reading for theological students, and many which were reprinted repeatedly in 1950s and 1960s.[30]

Most of the early books published by the Society were written in the Chinese literary style, not accessible to most ordinary Chinese. The time came when the Society could not sell many of these early publications. As Albert surveyed the piles of unsold religious books in the basement where they were stored, he began to wonder if the Society was really responding to the actual needs of readers in China and to the work of the various Missions. So began a series of books designed for schools and colleges written by himself and then translated into

Chinese, which became popular and sold well. They were written in the language of the common people.

By now, Albert was an excellent Chinese scholar and linguist, well read, and able to express himself clearly in current Chinese. Working in close cooperation with Chinese colleagues, he achieved faithful and idiomatic translation. The growing list of original works from his pen reveals not only scholarship but an appreciation of the needs of ordinary people.

He experimented with the application of Western techniques in printing by using movable type, casting from matrices, cutting steel punches, and using printing machines.

Albert also believed standards in both general and theological education were low, and there was a need for a more highly trained Chinese ministry. He made arrangements with two universities to publish specially written theological handbooks. One further achievement at this time was of huge ecumenical significance, creating a lasting legacy. In 1937 came the first edition of *Hymns of Universal Praise,* a joint venture of six denominations and the most widely-used Chinese hymn book until recent times.

Albert's translations included Professor of Christian Dogmatics, David Cairns' [31] *The Reasonableness of the Christian Faith.* In his book of 250-pages, Dr Cairns seeks to show that the true explanation of Nature is not found in her glory, beauty, terror, and pain but "is behind and above her in the Unseen." Among other works Albert translated was the massive 450-pages of *The Story of Christ,* by Giovanni Papini,[32] from the Italian original.

Another translation venture directly from the Italian was Alessandro Manzoni's historical novel *I Promessi Sposi'* [33] *(The Betrothed).* Although it is a long book, Albert felt that it might "speak to the condition" of thoughtful young people in China from outside the context of direct Christian teaching, although this teaching is implicit in the story: "troubles come to everybody in this world, sometimes our own fault, sometimes through that of others."

Albert offered this manuscript to the Commercial Press, the largest publishing house in the Far East at that time, and who a few years before had been unwilling to give shelf-room to books from the Society. Now, to his surprise, they agreed to publish *I Promessi Sposi.*

Original works authored by Albert included *The Story of Jesus,* and *Chinese Versions of the Bible,* published in 1933 in English, and numerous commentaries on books, and Church Histories. The accurate Chinese style of his writing was admired by the Chinese themselves. Some said he was a second Li Ti-rno-tai (Timothy Richard) and no praise could have been higher.[34]

Albert's 20 years of teaching Chinese students enabled him to approach his material from their point of view, so that a Chinese lady, herself an author, picking up one of his books, said: "This was never written by a foreigner." The English version of *The Story of Jesus* opens thus:

"Nearly 2000 years ago, in the western part of Asia, in a country smaller than the smallest Chinese Province, there lived a man who turned the world upside down. The name of the country was Palestine, and that of the man – Jesus."

This book was followed by three more volumes, concerning Christianity, and how it spread. The last one, *A Short History of Christianity*, went into twelve editions before Albert left the Society in 1937, followed by further editions in 1948, 1953 and 1965 and is still on sale on the Chinese Christian Literature Society website.[35]

Albert was amazed to find in the late 1930s that a *Chinese Anthology of Modern Prose* included three chapters from his translation of *Chinese Versions of the Bible*, offered to the public as examples of good modern style.[36] "This process in the evolution of modern Chinese is most important as one indication of the changed attitude brought about by the 1911 Revolution," concluded Albert. [37] The influence of Albert and the Society also is, surely, a factor.

But Albert's work was halted mid-stride by illness. His circular letter written in December 1930 mentions what he calls "chronic dysentery" which proved to be the dreaded Eastern intestinal disease known as sprue. At that time its cause was not known and treatment largely experimental. He returned to England before the worst of the summer heat, in May 1931, looking very thin. The Christian Literature Society waited on his return in order to discuss with him the proposed merger of the ancient Religious Tract Society, founded in 1799, with the Society.

He responded well to a dietary treatment regime, and was much fitter in a few months. He returned to Shanghai in September 1932, and remained until 1937.

An earlier task Albert had organised was a campaign to rehouse the Society. It was proposed to build a nine-storey building in the city's centre.

Designed by architect Laszlo Hudec,[38] the building is very near the Bund and the teeming life of the waterfront. The first seven floors were to be let as offices, using the income from rents to repay the bank overdraft. Most of the staff were to be on the top two floors, and part of the ground floor to house a bookshop and the mailing department. Some deplored the proposal and said that the Society would be financially ruined, but the project went through to completion in 1932 and quickly proved to be viable.

With a new building and a rejuvenated General Secretary, forward planning was now possible and the next five years saw an astonishing expansion on every side of the Society's work.[39] Albert's last years in Shanghai were action-packed. What he carried out was immeasurable in its far-reaching effects and his reputation quickly grew.

The work on magazines designed for a wide variety of readers, from children, women with a limited education, to university students, was gathered into one place. As well as his literary work, Albert was in demand as a preacher and speaker at important Shanghai occasions.

The distinctive and imposing Christian Literature Society building on Yuanmingyuan Road.

When the opportunity came to set up a Christian Radio Station – the first station anywhere in the world to offer its listeners a whole programme of religious content in various languages for several hours a day – the Society's new building provided the perfect setting, both within for a studio, and outside with its towering height for a radio-mast.

The Christian Literature Society Building where the Shanghai Christian Broadcasting Station was located.

The Chinese government granted official permission for the station, and leading Chinese firms and banks gave financial support to maintain its operation by the Shanghai Christian Broadcasting Association housed in the Society's building.

Albert had great influence on the direction of the station's policy and encouraged the widest possible use of the service. The impact of the radio station was immediate, helping Chinese and the many foreigners in Shanghai and beyond to know of the Society's existence. Letters of appreciation were received from across China.

The daily programme was almost entirely religious. Although it was a Chinese language station, an innovation included an evangelical service each evening in other languages – Russian, Japanese, German, English and French.

In addition to the weekly service in French, Albert gave a weekly series of talks on various themes – 12 talks on a simple presentation of the Christian religion, 11 talks of a devotional character on the development of the Christian life, and a set of talks on some of the best-known Christian hymns. "In this I secured the co-operation of a Shanghai business man who used to belong to a Yorkshire choir. He sings a verse or two of each hymn introduced."

Although Albert said he avoided politics and political expression, he was sensitive to the impact of his words. In the many special addresses or when leading a sermon, "I can assure you that I appreciate this opportunity, and prepare my talks with the utmost care, for I know that some Chinese in high positions are in the habit of listening in, not only in Shanghai, but in other cities as well. Who knows how much some word or some sentence might mean when it falls on soil prepared for it?"

Albert knew that the Chinese themselves realised that the 1911 Revolution had opened a new door and that 'China is at the Parting of the Ways' and the future of China, for good or ill, was within the fellowship of nations and they had a contribution to make to it. "This is clear from the discussions, in private and public, and from the numberless speeches, articles and books of the post-revolution era." [40] Albert was hopeful for progress in the material sphere in the context of the ultimate outcome of the "right relationship between man and God". For him the main question was how much or how little of the past should be conserved or adapted; and, how much or how little of Western civilisation should be embodied in the life of New China.

Broadcasting took up a good deal of his time. The original 150 kilowatts (kW) station was replaced with a new 1,000kW transmitter installed in 1936, with the hope that the Society's messages would reach the farthest limits of China. At the time, it was the largest transmitting power among China's domestic private radio stations.[41]

The strengthened radio station was opened by Madame Chiang Kai Shek, wife of China's president, who addressed a Christian message to the nation. Both the president and his wife had become Christians after witnessing the behaviour of missionaries under persecution.

When several hospitals and mission schools were looted and destroyed, General Chiang appealed for volunteers to help the Red Cross work. Much to his surprise, the very doctors whose hospitals had been burned and houses destroyed volunteered to help. He could not understand this at all, and sought for explanations. "This is exactly what Christianity is," Chiang was told. This impressed so much that they asked for baptism.

Throughout this last term of service, Albert lived in a room in the new Christian Literature Society building, which meant he had no expenses getting to work. He fed on Korean apples, bought by the crate, cheese, brown bread, butter and milk. On Sundays he often had a meal with friends, frequently at the house of the Mission Treasurer, Adam Black, whose dwelling was the nearest thing to a home for him in those years. He never had another attack of sprue during the five years which he spent in Shanghai after the onset of the illness, nor in the 36 years of his life after leaving Shanghai.

He also wrote four letters every week to his family in England throughout his years in Shanghai, usually four sides of quarto paper to his wife (none of which remain) and anything between one and two sides to each of his children separately.

Albert's work in Shanghai's prison – "I had a difficult time"

Every Sunday for nearly 10 years, Albert met with prisoners condemned to death in the Shanghai gaol, where his excellent colloquial Chinese and long friendships with Chinese people made it possible for him to get in touch as few other foreigners could hope to do. Their furious or troubled faces stare out from the descriptions written by Albert in his quarterly letters to the Baptist Church in Canterbury: [42]

June, 1930: On Easter Day, in spite of the sunshine and the thought of the Resurrection, I had a difficult time. To begin with, the first thing I saw as I walked along the corridor was that the first three cells were empty; the man with the red face who used to roar with laughter, he had gone; so had the young boy, with a surprised look full of fear on his face, who had broken down when I had spoken to him of his home people; so had an impassive high-chested fellow, who would listen quietly enough, but who would then pace restlessly up and down the little cell, while I could hear his chains rattling against the floor, as I was talking to the next man. Further on there was another empty cell, the one where the smooth-spoken man of some culture was locked up. All these had been executed on the Wednesday before Easter, and naturally one does not think of such things with a light heart.

But in another cell, I had a worse shock, though of a different kind. In that cell there was a young man to whom I had often spoken before, but who had proved dull and obstinate. On Easter morning however he proved to be in a more open frame of mind, and he began to ask me a few questions. He wanted to know whether the story of Christ was true, especially whether the miracle of feeding the five thousand had really happened. He seemed to have something on his mind about it and determined not to leave any point in obscurity.

Did Christ have five loaves large enough to be cut into 5,000 pieces, or had there really been a miracle of multiplication? Then he passed on to another question as to whether such miracles had anything to do with us now. The expression he used was forceful and might be translated thus: Are these miracles and especially this one, merely fairy tales with a fine teaching given to help us, or are they actual facts meant to show a power which can work today in our world? I told him that I believed the miracles of Christ were part of his message, every bit as true and real and possible as his teaching. Then he let out at me, and I will try to render as faithfully as I can what he said. He said it, not in an angry way at all, but in a sort of half earnest, half resentful, hopeless way, as of a man who has lost out on the struggle of life. "When I was 'outside'," he began, "I had read about these miracles of Jesus, and I was struck by this one of the feedings of the five thousand, because I myself often had no food, and I did not want my wife and children to suffer hunger. You know, when one's body is hungry, the soul does not seem to matter so much. I prayed to God. I prayed to God in the name of this very Jesus who multiplied the loaves and fishes, to give me bread, but He didn't. How can you expect me to believe that it works at all? Why do you tell me these things are true? I can't believe now, whatever you may say, because I myself know that it is not true. I prayed to God, but God did not answer me."

Albert: "I looked at him helplessly, for I realised, how deep his experience had been, and I had no answer. At least, I had no answer that I could put in words, and I silently sought for guidance, lest I should leave this man without any help. I got as near him as I could, almost touching him, and I told him that I fully understood how he must feel about it, and that I could not tell him why God had not given him the bread he asked for. I tried to show that sometimes God does not answer prayer for reasons that we don't understand at the time, and I begged him not to allow this experience of his to take away the realization that God was very near, in this cell with us."

Albert listened quietly and left him smiling, but it was a smile that seemed to say: "You may believe these things yourself, but I know that God does not help men."

January, 1933: I invariably urge these men to trust God – a difficult thing for us all at times – and to pray not for themselves only but for the "aged lady" or the "old man" at home, as well as for the children left without a father's support. This particular prisoner told me that his father had come to Shanghai, to wait here for the execution, that he might take the body away and bury it at home. "He sells vegetables for a living," the man informed me, with agony in his voice and tears streaming down his cheeks.

I want to say to those of you who find it hard to keep up your support of mission work, that there are out here men and women who would be without hope but for the message of Christ. It is true that life is not easy and claims are many, but whatever you give up don't let go of this great privilege of sharing this work of telling of the love of Jesus."

August 1933: A few Sundays ago, a Chinese pastor came with me; he himself was so moved that it was difficult to get him away when we have to leave at 10.30. I was standing by his side telling him that the time was up, and he would try to finish what he was saying to the prisoner, but couldn't. The hungry eye of the fellow behind the bars showed that he was taking in every word. In the end, the pastor, moved as much as the poor wretch, said to him: "come, let us pray together, I don't know what else to do for you." That prayer went home. The Indian warders, standing close by, who had been grinning because of my unavailing efforts to remind the pastor that it was time to go, saw that something was happening, and a look of wonder replaced the grin on their bearded faces.

Nearly all the men under sentence of death have been given a copy of the New Testament – a gift of the British and Foreign Bible Society. It makes a world of difference. One does not know, of course, what is going on in those souls, embittered by the fight for daily bread, and words are often but poor means for the communication of ideas; yet, in contact with men who are facing death, one learns to understand something of human thought which is not revealed in the intercourse of ordinary life, and I am convinced that some of these men have come to believe in Jesus Christ.

In a testimony to the work of the Chinese Christians who visited the prison with him, Albert said: "It is not a work which brings profit or glory to anyone. It is not part of anybody's official duty; it is not advertised; there is no elaborate planning; there are no reports; yet these men came Sunday after Sunday, some of them from a long distance, at their own expense. There is no glory in such work, except the glory which comes from visiting the prisoners for Christ's sake."

"I never get out of the place (the prison), into the busy street full of barrows, rickshaws, trams, buses and what not, without saying to myself: "This is a hard world for some people. But for the goodness of God, I might be one of these men."

Clearly, Albert's prison visits were pretty gruesome, and he felt strongly about their importance and the role he played. His compassion, humility and his toughness and his energy is reflected in his accounts of prison visits.

Last days in China

As Albert prepared to leave China, his dream was that a Chinese take charge of the Society who would work up a constructive and varied programme, seeking out the best speakers – "Here is a challenge".

Albert was in Shanghai at the outbreak of hostilities between China and Japan. Poor China, was his reaction. Most foreign residents clearly indicated what they thought would happen: How long would China be able to last? Most hardly dared to suggest it would be longer than a few months.

But Albert foresaw a different outcome. "The unexpected resistance is an indication of the change that the 1911 Revolution had brought about." [43] There was the fact that the Chinese immediately set their hands to caring for the wounded and homeless, with Chinese Christians taking a leading part.

Albert recorded that a Chinese girl managed to take a Chinese flag into a Shanghai building cut off by a vastly superior force of Japanese on three sides, which was seen next day waving over the building in which they were besieged.

There was the resistance put up by thousands of Chinese behind the lines; when we speak of 'occupied' China, it is different to whole countries that were occupied by the Germans in Europe, but is only in 'zones' along railway lines, rivers and in the vicinity of large cities. The Chinese military response to the Japanese army was based on guerrilla tactics of harassment and surprise. According to old standards, the able general in China was the one who made a successful escape out of the north gate of the city while his enemy came in by the south gate. "A deep change has taken place in this direction," Albert wrote. He realised this personally during the struggle of the Japanese to take Shanghai: "Night after night, a Chinese colleague and I watched from the roof of the Christian Literature Society building, he would pull my coat and say excitedly, 'Look, there it is – the flag is still waving.'"

China also organized a guerrilla industry, building hundreds of small factories which were light, flexible and mobile, and which could operate far inland. The factories produced a bewildering variety of goods that war-torn China needed – from candles and light bulbs to boilers, small boats and spare parts for railway engines. Around 50,000 workers produced goods valued at $6 million each month – everything which was needed and was not being made in the bombed-out factories in Shanghai, Fuzhou, Tianjin and Wuhan was being made in the countryside beyond the reach of Japanese bombers, "by an energized, optimistic, and newly purposeful Chinese rural workforce." [44]

One and all Chinese feel bitter against Japan, wrote Albert. "I know that their heart is full of hate. They face me with conditions in Europe, [45] and it would take an abler diplomat than I am to cover my sense of shame!"

Albert returned to England in 1937, having survived the first air-raids on Shanghai by the Japanese, and a typhoon in Hong Kong harbour which damaged the vessel, the "Conte Verde," in which he had begun his return journey. It was too badly damaged to proceed on the voyage. Luckily, he was able to get a berth on a German ship, the "Gneisenau," going to Genoa. From there it was easy to visit his home in Torre Pellice, on his way back to London.

Chapter 5: FROM VIOLENT REVOLUTIONS TO PEACEFUL EVOLUTION?

"GOVERNING a large state is like boiling a small fish," said Lao Tzu, a famous Chinese thinker in the 1st century BC. Why?

On his return to London from Shanghai in 1937, Albert had not finished with China – far from it.

After a sad but temporary disruption to his freedom as Britain entered World War II,[46] Albert was appointed as a war-time postal census officer in Liverpool to inspect mail to and from China and Italy.

Eventually, he was asked to join the British Broadcasting Corporation (BBC) with the job of "Supervisor in the Chinese section" – a role he held for 14 years (until 1962, close to age 80).

Albert's work with the BBC involved preparing and translating the English script of broadcasts to China, with due regard to the special dialects, interests and aptitudes of Chinese staff; checking the Chinese versions, and then monitoring the broadcast itself. This was highly skilled work, for no one knew better than he how easy it was to let slip a double-meaning which would convey more to a Chinese listener than an English one. He made a dictionary of proper-names in Chinese characters of people often in the news, and this had a subtle importance in assuring that British people did not lose face in Chinese eyes as a result of their leaders being labelled with names expressed in Chinese characters apparently innocently, but which might also contain an insult.

His writing on China continued, including in 1945, *A Maker of Modern China,* written as a memorial on the hundredth anniversary of Dr Richard's birth. In this book Albert looks at China at the close of World War II and gives his final verdict of the impact of the 1911 Revolution on Chinese society and the influence of religion.

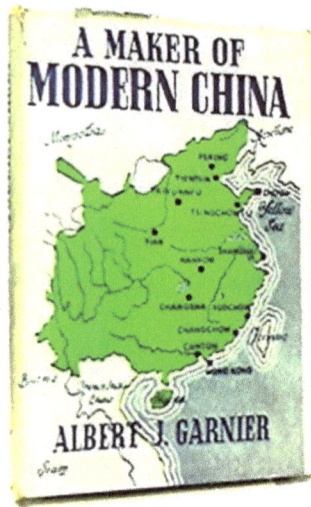

A MAKER OF MODERN CHINA

ALBERT J. GARNIER

Albert asked: How far is the 'New China' likely to draw its inspiration from its ancient faiths of Confucianism, Taoism and Buddhism, or from modern Christianity (Protestantism), or a system such as Communism? [47]

The change in China since 1911 was exemplified in a variety of ways:

◊ **The invasion of China by Japan (1935-36):** Around 60 million people migrated from various parts of China to the Far West so that they still might be free, and took with them their industrial plants and universities. They tackled with vigour, in spite of military operations, the problem of illiteracy and they experimented with industrial co-operatives. Under the stress of circumstances, scholars and common people were thrown together as never before, learning to know one another better with mutual advantage, and, in spite of rifts still existing, a larger measure of national unity than ever before was achieved.

◊ **The lifting of the spoken language of the people to the dignity of a literature:** The change came about through a Chinese leader, Hu Shih, who Albert knew and often met in the late 1920s and early 1930s. Hu Shih is known as the first promoter of vernacular Chinese as the modern literary language. This brought about dramatic changes in literary as well as social norms, which Albert successfully applied in his many writings.

◊ Albert saw an equivalence with what Dante did for Italian with his *Divine Comedy,* and Luther did for German with his translation of the Bible into the vernacular, and, to a certain extent, what Calvin did for French with his *Institutes (of the Christian Religion)*, what a host of Chinese writers have done, and are still doing, for Chinese.

◊ **The role and position of women in China:** With the disappearance of bound feet, women in China have developed a new physique and status. "They are no longer little more than (just) a child-bearer to her lord. She has become his equal, his friend and companion, his partner, often his inspiration and guide – for good or evil." No one who has not witnessed the change is in a position to appreciate its depth, Albert wrote.

◊ "It is difficult not to see, in all these changes, something more vital than a mere revolution to overthrow a foreign Dynasty. There are in it the elements of a re-orientation of ideas, of a re-birth."

Albert could see the fruit of work begun by Dr Richard, and continued on by himself, "unrecognized though it may be on the surface."

"Even I can feel the thrill of having witnessed the re-birth of a mighty nation," Albert wrote in 1945.[48]

The main questions under debate, including by Albert, was how much or how little of the past should be conserved, and, if necessary, adapted; and how much or how little of Western civilization should be embodied in the life of the New China.[49]

In dealing with this debate, London-based journalist, Hsiao Ch'ien, urged Chinese not to allow the 'machine' to kill the 'soul'.[50] He wrote two books, *The Dragon's Beard,* supporting ancient Chinese civilization, while his *Blue Prints* stands for modern progress along lines of the machine of industry.

Albert was convinced: Should Chinese place their faith exclusively in civilization that finds its chief expression in the "machine", neither Confucianism, Buddhism, nor Communism will save them. "They will do no more than add one competitor on the world's markets, with all the possibilities for future wars that this would involve, and they will lose also much that has been of value in their ancient culture and civilization."[51]

It is the 'machine' which is threatening to kill the soul of the West; and it was primarily to save the soul of China that Protestant missionaries (like Dr Richard, Garnier and others) "thought, and preached, and wrote, and lived, and died". That was Albert's conclusion.

What has happened since 1945? How is Confucianism and Christianity (Protestantism and Catholicism) faring in today's China? What of Communism? And what can be said about the legacy created by Albert and other Protestant missionaries?

After the Chinese Communist victory in 1949,[52] Christianity's fortunes in China seemed doomed. China officially became an atheist state. Religion was suppressed, and the Chinese government expelled all missionaries in 1950-51, confiscated churches and brought pressure on Christians. The Christian Literature Society had become the biggest Christian literature distribution centre in Asia, and coupled with the impact of the radio station, the Society had created a lasting influence that was reflected in the make-up of the new Chinese government.

While the Society terminated its activities, re-emerging in Hong Kong with a new name, paradoxically, Protestantism and Catholicism, were recognized as official religions. A Religious Affairs Bureau was established to oversee all religious activities in China, and manage the five recognized religions – Buddhism, Taoism, Islam, Protestantism, Catholicism.

Religious practice in China became, and continues to be complicated. All religions must register under one of the five accepted denominations in order to legally worship, or face criminal charges if caught worshipping without registration.

In 1954, the Chinese Congress stipulated that all adult citizens have freedom of religious belief, but uncertainty remained as to how religious practice would be treated under the Marxist ideology that China followed at that time – given Marxism's stance against religion.

All aspects of religious life were managed – appointments, selection of clergy, and interpretation of doctrine. To register as state-sanctioned Protestant and Catholic organisations, religious leaders must receive training to 'adapt' doctrine to government and Chinese Communist Party thinking.

From 1966 to 1979, religious persons of all faiths suffered attacks and persecution. Albert's optimistic future for China looked impossible under Mao Zedong, the founder of the People's Republic of China, and he was reminded of the persecutions by the Catholics of the Waldensians suffered for centuries by his ancestors.[53]

During the Cultural Revolution, no churches or other religious bodies could operate. Protestants and Catholics continued to exist, but they suffered grievously. The influence of Buddhism and Taoism was reduced, China's leaders believing that ancient Chinese traditions and beliefs were the main cause of China's decline. By the middle of the 20th century, half of China's temples had been destroyed.

Confucianism received fierce criticism from both liberals and Marxists. Hu Shih advocated overthrowing 'The House of Confucius'. He was convinced that a stable political settlement could be achieved only after the social patterns and intellectual assumptions of the past had been swept away. He sought to push China out into the march of world history. Mao Zedong, also repeatedly denounced Confucius and Confucianism.

Both Hu Shih and Mao were ultimately at odds with many in China. Despite these fierce criticisms and harsh persecutions, even today, as we will see, both Confucius and Christian, especially Protestant ideas remain in the minds and hearts of many Chinese people.

Albert despaired, but he believed that Mao Zedong's 'reforms' would vanish (unlike the language reform of Hu Shih, which would remain).

From 1976, things changed. Thinking and policy was revised. Under Deng Xiaoping's open-door policy, as well as stimulating an economic resurgence, many Mao-era bans were lifted, including the ban on religions and religious practice. Protestant and Roman Catholic churches were resurrected, and in varied ways 'silent' house-churches testified that an underground church movement had been dramatically growing. Confucianism and other ancient faiths (Buddhism and Taoism) also re-emerged.

All this despite the Marxist ideology insisting on the eventual demise of religion. Instead, with the rise in living standards and reduced influence of ancient Buddhism and Taoism, it opened the door for greater Protestant expansion.

But to what extent? As Albert wrote in 1945, anyone who is acquainted with China knows the danger of prophesying what China will do.[54] It is therefore, not in a spirit of dogmatic certainty that I write the rest of this chapter, but as an observer lucky enough to have undertaken assignments in many parts of Asia, Europe, America and Africa. China is its own world. It is different.

In the event, in 1987, I visited Beijing, Guizhou (Guiyang and Anshun), Guangzhou, Shenzhen and Jiulong.[55] The experience was like having five or six different appetisers and missing the main course. It is foolhardy to generalise from such a limited visit, and yet I agree with Albert that being Chinese is an evolving attitude of mind, a spiritual concept that is linked into the oldest of their ancestors and the newest building block in their land.

Visiting Shanghai meant coming into contact with self-confident people, immersed in the pleasures of a sustained period of peace and independence, enjoying plentiful and cheap food for the first time in more than a century, and exploring opportunities to save and buy modern consumer goods. As I wrote:

Department stores are packed with people making first-time purchases. The incongruities are endless. Millions of bicycles clog streets, bells ringing, but riders in no real hurry nonetheless secure in the knowledge that this is their patch.

Bicycles can carry the world. One heads towards me, a wicker cage on the handle bar contains three quacking ducks. On the bar sits a son or daughter, perhaps two years old, smiling and licking ice cream. Father moves the bike at a steady pace, and as it passes a large box strapped on the bike's back is fully visible; its large label proclaiming "HITACHI". It is a television set.

Like families across the rest of the developed world, most Chinese families watch television most evenings, and especially China's nationwide news programme which started about a year ago. Other popular programmes are sport, the Beijing Opera, classical music and stories. Excerpts from "The Dream of the Red Chamber", a Chinese literary classic, are top viewing.

Television has added a new dimension to Chinese life. It helps underline why modernisation won't be reversed. It can't be.

My host (but not her children) attends one of 10 churches in Shanghai which have reopened in the last few years. Real independence has come only in the wake of snipping the ideological and allied status with the Soviet Union. And the cultural revolution is regarded as just a blip on China's new history, a wobble as China has stood up and tried to run its own affairs.

Elsewhere I was told that the period 1966-79 was among the darkest in mankind's history. The scale of suffering was not (yet) fully comprehended outside China; more than 100 million people had been physically transported, untold millions disappearing. Many middle aged and elderly Chinese had been "marked" by their own children. It was a decade which, in hindsight, had served only to make young people more sensitive to the need for China's modernisation, but by a planned, peaceful evolution not by way of destructive revolution.

With reference to Chinese Leader Deng's dictum, the aim of change was to create "socialism with Chinese characteristics".

There is a tranquil confidence, a passive style, but a thirst to learn. Bookshops were always packed with young people reading and buying textbooks, a lot published recently. They weren't buying Marx, Engels or political tracts, though plenty were available; rather, the interest was in computers, electronics, genetics, evolution, and economics.

The aim of China's leadership in the mid-1980s is to have evolved by 2050 to a modern, market-led social democracy whose standard of living matches if not is ahead of other advanced nations.

It won't be a Marxist society. It won't be capitalist. It will be uniquely Chinese, a new society evolved on a prescription of Chinese values but incorporating the best of what the other half of the world has to offer.

A constant in many of the discussions was the belief that China needed to see sustained peace into the next century if its reforms were to succeed.

China had been in turmoil virtually since the 1840s, when foreign powers gained effective control, and the Boxer rebellion of 1900 when 'foreign devil' control began to unwind. After the shambles of the Mao years and cultural revolution, China was now anxious for a long period of peace so it could build a stable and competitive economy, was a persistent theme.

The demand for improved economic standards in China is now set clearly on the target of "catch up" with the advanced nations. If allowed to operate, China's economic progress will generate sufficient momentum to maintain an upward trend in living standards for the foreseeable future. The increased production of nutrition and growth of industry will ensure economic expansion supporting China's demand to the world that, with the rest of Asia, it will act as the agent of a new historical trend.

In the 1980s, China's leadership was obviously trying to move China away from rigid economic planning. The proof was everywhere.

Market-led economic zones like Shenzhen near Hong Kong were the catalyst for improved living standards for many people. Agricultural reforms, involving free-market elements, had greatly boosted production and income for the rural 80 percent of the population. Food self-sufficiency had been achieved, and the emphasis turned to boosting protein intake.

Put another way, China was starting to say to the world: We are half the world's population, we must for our own survival raise our standards of life; help us if you will, but please don't obstruct us or exploit us.

Where China goes in the 21st century, so goes the world? This question is the outcome of detached observation during the visit and logical analysis: A new China-centred civilization will evolve because it is implicit in the continuity of the (Chinese) historical process.

From my years in journalism, I know how risky it is to form opinions on the basis of just a brief visit. However, during my time in China, I was privileged to have some extensive – and sometimes frank – private exchanges with senior officials in different regions of China.

The firm impression I was given, from interviews in all parts of the country but particularly Beijing, was that reforms would continue indefinitely. There was no going back. However, there was a debate about the pace of change. It was too fast for some, and too slow for others. And the future could see upheavals and power struggles, but never a turning back on the reform programme.

Perhaps the best proof of China's determination to continue the reforms was the resolution by the central committee in October 1986 not only that the economic reforms would continue, but that they would be locked in by political and spiritual reforms. A senior official gave me an outline of the overall objective:

◊ In the economic reform the essence is to loosen central authority power to the grassroots and regions, and "enliven" the economy. The two key policies at the moment were to decentralise control and remove price control on non-stable items. Steel, coal, timber, cement and machinery were mentioned. "We are encouraging people to break the monopoly hold and become production driven."

◊ Reform of the political system was "the hot topic" of the moment. The core of the reform was how to democratise politics but within a framework of public ownership. There were several aspects; too much bureaucracy and low efficiency; the personal power system of the 28 million cadres; legal reform, including price and factory laws.

◊ Spiritual reform was the capping stone, and concerned with ideological and cultural aspects. The idea was to lift out the essence of China's ideological and cultural "way" or tradition and absorb into it the best of Western (or non-Chinese) cultures, either historic or current. Public ownership was still a key concept, but was being redefined in non-Marxist terms.

◊ I was referred to a *Xinhua* commentary by Ban Yue Tan, a noted Government-approved commentator: "Marx and Lenin were great men. The Marxist-Leninist theory they founded has displayed great vitality and stood the test of time. However, it should be acknowledged that the field of vision of a great man, whoever he is, will always be limited. There were no cars in Marx's time, Engels never went in an aircraft and Lenin never saw a film with sound. Let us review the history. Following the passing of time, we have now entered the age of electronics and space. Let us look at the world."

◊ By the mid-1980s the Chinese had apparently decided not to rely on Marxist-styled Communism as their inspiration for the building up of the 'New China'. Instead, the driving force was Deng's 'socialism with Chinese characteristics'. What, then, are the chances of 'New China' adopting protestant thinking as envisioned by Albert in 1945?

Or, why is *'governing a large state like boiling a small fish'*? Lao Tzu's ANSWER: *'Because a small fish can be spoiled simply by being handled'*. Is this, then, a consideration in President Xi Jinping's planning to adopt a traditional "way" which absorbs into it the best of Western spiritual thinking? We shall see.

PART TWO: **ALBERT'S WALDENSIAN ANCESTRY AND EXTENDED FAMILY**

Chapter 6:   ARRIVAL IN THE ISRAEL OF THE COTTIAN ALPS

PRAGELATO ('Icy Meadow') **1265**: A small, isolated and often snow-bound village located high on the Italian side of the Cottian Alps, close to the French border. The Garnier family arrive from Lyon, France.[56] Few details of their circumstances are known other than that they were Waldensians, one of the two great heretical sects of the Middle Ages, the other being Catharism.[57]

The history of the Waldensians is a long and complicated story of faith and survival.[58] Two different histories persist to the present day. According to Waldensian records, they are descendants of the apostles, carrying the torch passed on to them by the first-century Christian church. Seeing the importance of education, they built a small stone 'college' in the Angronga valley, under the shadow of the ancient site of the Waldensian *Pra Del Torno* temple,[59] for the purpose of learning and study. Known as the *College of the Barbas* ('Uncles'),[60] it still stands today as a testimony to these early missionaries.

Albert's home, *Fournasa*, was close by. Together with two or three other churches in the Waldensian valleys dating from at least the 16th century they form in their severe simplicity, in Albert's view, a striking contrast to the newer buildings of a more ornamental style.

It is undisputed that in 1532, at the Synod of Chanforan, held under a tree above the hillside from Albert's house, the Waldensians decided to throw in their lot with the new Protestant movements in Germany led by Luther. In other words, the Waldensians already upheld what the Reformation proclaimed.

A second, populist history asserts that the Waldensians originated with a French leader, a Lyon merchant, Peter Waldo, (or *Valdes* in French) [61], who converted to the religious life in the early 1170s. Waldo formed a movement that was excommunicated in 1184.

From about 1080 until 1320, Lyon was part of the Holy Roman Empire[62]. The Catholic bishops ran the city, pursuing a succession of inquisitions. Through this period, the city suffered from 12 plague epidemics, numerous floods, famines, and armed groups spreading terror.

Historical texts indicate Garniers were involved in the Great Inquisition of urban elites that characterized the mid-1200s: some trials feature Catharism and others Waldensians, while local power struggles between bishop and secular 'elites' dominated. The texts of trials mention "Garnier senior" and the "Garnier family" without specifying what the substance of the trial was about.

But later texts indicate that Garniers were early converts to Waldensian beliefs, and subsequent generations maintained this.

Waldensian beliefs allowed ordinary men and women to read the Bible and to preach. They were innovations unacceptable to the Catholic Church, with the reading and interpretation of sacred texts strictly reserved for the Catholic clergy.[63]

This central importance of the Bible is physically demonstrated in every Waldensian church building, by means of an open copy of the Bible placed facing the congregation, on the communion table, which stands below the pulpit. The first translation of the Bible into French direct from Hebrew and Greek texts, and one of the first of any translations into a vernacular, was made at the request of the Waldensian Synod of 1532.

The study of the Bible meant that education was cherished and sought for the children of Waldensians. This gave Albert his language expertise at an early age.

Another Waldensian belief is the separation of the Church and State, that is, full secularity. Waldensians became convinced that the church would lose its spiritual life if it became wealthy, privileged and powerful in the world. When Emperor Constantine made Catholicism the state religion in the 4th century, the Waldensians saw it as a compromise and the start of the church's downfall. They believed that Scripture was the true and final authority, not the Catholic Church.

Waldensians had no problem entering municipal roles, some getting elected to important leadership positions. However, most preferred to remain on the margins of political life, believing in remaining poor and distrusting human authorities.

By 1586, Garniers had moved from Pragelato down the mountain valleys into the remote Bobbio Pellice[64] village at the head of the Val Pellice, some 10km from Torre Pellice at the entrance to the valley, and today the headquarters of the Waldensian movement.

During the 15th to 17th centuries Val Pellice and the surrounding valleys were scenes of terrible massacres. History tells that the Waldensians suffered 33 invasions into their valleys with the purpose of wiping them out, and getting them to convert to Catholicism. In every town in Piedmont, Waldensians were put to death. On one account, a relative, "Paul Garnier was slowly sliced to pieces."[65]

In April 1655, during the Piedmont Easter massacre, 3,000 people died on Mount Castelluzzo, near Bobbio Pellice. (See cover photograph & below.) Family tradition recounts that Marguerete Garnier was the person referred to by poet

John Milton in his 1655 Sonnet *On the Late Massacre in Piedmont* mentioning a 'mother with infant' being rolled down the cliff from Castelluzzo.[66] It's a sheer drop of over 500 feet. Half way down the face is a ledge where people hid. You cannot see the ledge from the cliff top or bottom but they now have iron spikes in the rock to climb down to it.

On the Late Massacre in Piedmont

Avenge, O Lord, thy slaughtered Saints, whose bones

Lie scattered on the Alpine mountains cold;

Even them who kept thy truth so pure of old,

When all our fathers worshiped stocks and stones,

Forget not: in thy book record their groans

Who were thy sheep, and in their ancient fold

Slain by the bloody Piedmontese, that rolled

Mother with infant down the rocks. Their moans

The vales redoubled to the hills, and they

To heaven. Their martyred blood and ashes sow

O'er all the Italian fields, where still doth sway

The triple Tyrant; that from these may grow

A hundredfold, who, having learnt thy way,

Early may fly the Babylonian woe.

Mt Castelluzzo, site of the 1655 massacre, dominates over Torre Pellice.

But the massacre was far from the end of the attempt by the Duke of Savoy to implement the wish of the Catholic Church to eradicate Protestantism from the valleys. A resistance campaign began. Joshua Janavel (1617-1690), a member of the Waldensian Church, was among the accidental heroes created by the massacre. Born in Rorà, a hillside village across the Val Pellice from Albert's home in Angrogna, Janavel was a relatively prosperous farmer until his life took a sharp turn in 1655 when the Duke launched his military operation against the Waldensian population.

Janavel was involved in the Piedmontese Easter fighting, and in another battle led the defence of Rorà and succeeded in repelling the Savoyard assault. For the courage which he displayed at this battle, he became known as 'the Lion of Rora' and 'the captain of the valleys'. The resistance did not endure. The Waldensians were defeated in the nearby Valley of Germanasca and Janavel was forced into exile.

However, despite threats against his family and a bounty on his head, Janavel soon returned to reorganize the Waldensian insurgents, together with Barthelemy Jahier, a fellow captain and hero of the Waldensian community to this day. [67]

Janavel and Jahier led various actions leading up to when Savoyard forces attacked Angrogna, Albert's home locality. The Waldensians weathered the initial assault and managed to counterattack, but during the counterattack Janavel was gravely wounded.

Janavel continued to lead the underground Waldensian resistance. Over the following years he mounted a number of guerrilla attacks against Savoyard forces, and his house in Rora served as a base of operations and general quarters for the insurgency. The duchy punished him with banishment and a death sentence. Jahier was eventually killed with fifty of his companions, victims of an ambush near the village of Osasco, near Pinerolo.

On 6 July 1663 the Savoyards again attacked Angrogna, but were defeated. The Waldensian community desired an end to war, and agreed to the conditions of the Duke of Savoy, which stipulated the exile of Janavel and his soldiers. A Waldensian synod disavowed Janavel, and he was sent into exile in Switzerland.

Janavel was welcomed as a Protestant hero, and maintained contacts with his home valley. Despite being under surveillance by the local authorities, as well as by Savoyard spies, he made at least two clandestine visits to the Val Pellice.

Meanwhile, bowing to international pressure, the Duke ended the campaign against the Waldensians and restored the status quo. It did not last.

In 1685, King Louis XIV of France rescinded the Edict which had provided a brief time of religious protection for the Waldensians. Once again, a widespread campaign began to purge the Waldensians and force them into Catholicism. Within three days, more than 8,000 had been imprisoned, and 2,000 killed.

Under intense pressure from Protestant nations, the Duke of Savoy (Victor Amadeus, and nephew of Louis XIV), finally agreed in January 1687 to perpetual exile for the survivors. Of 2,700 who began the 130km mid-winter trek from Bobbio Pellice over the Alps into Switzerland, only 2,490 actually reached Geneva; a "Jean" Garnier is listed among a group of 800 'moving skeletons' who arrived. Garnier recovered, and two years later returned to Bobbio Pellice as a hero.[68]

Once in exile, the Swiss were unable to convince the Waldensians to make permanent settlements. Together with Janavel, the Waldensian refugees began actively planning a mass return, a trek which became known as the Glorious Return of 1689. By this time Janavel was too old to take part personally, but he played a prominent role as an organizer; notably, he drafted the military orders governing the group's conduct during the operation.[69]

On 17 August 1689, a commando force began the 'Glorious Return.' The troop lost a third of its thousand-man force who began the return journey.[70] By May 1690, just 300 Waldensian troops remained. Arrayed against them were

4,000 French Catholic troops with canons. The final assault was delayed by a storm and then by dense fog. When the French prepared for their final assault the next morning, the Waldensians were nowhere to be found. During the night, guided by a local familiar with the area, and under cover of the dense fog, they had made what seemed an impossible descent and were miles away.

After further inconclusive skirmishes, a few days later, the Duke of Savoy, based in Torino, severed his alliance with France and joined with England and Austria. For political reasons, it seems, the exiles were invited to come home. The vacillating Duke needed these intrepid mountain-tough Waldensians to help protect his border against the French.

The Waldensians had prevailed, winning a series of battles and possession of their land and churches, even if this provoked the irate protests of Pope Innocent XII.

The 'Glorious Return' had set the scene for successive generations of Waldensians to live and practice in the 'perfect tranquility' of their valley, while, at the same time, receiving a high level of education through a system of alpine schools developed by English entrepreneurs.

In 1848, Waldensians, including the Garnier family in Bobbio Pellice, were granted full rights of Italian citizenship. For the first time in centuries, Waldensians could acquire land, hold public office, and choose the profession they wished, and their children could qualify for higher education, and by the end of the 19th century the community had a negligible percentage of illiterate people.

But the declaration failed to provide greater religious freedom. In 1875, when Alexis Muston, wrote a thesis on the Waldensians without the Catholic Church's official permission, he was taken to court and had to flee the country. His book, *The Israel of the Alps: A Complete History of the Waldenses of Piedmont and their Colonies,* provides perhaps the most significant history of the Waldensians from the time of their origins to their emancipation.

In 1929, Mussolini and the Catholic Church signed a Concordat which repudiated the notion of a free state. The Waldensian Church was only 'permitted', and all Protestants were suspect because they had contacts abroad and were known for their passion for liberty and their spirit of autonomy.[71] This edict would have a significant import during World War II and the strong Waldensian support, including by the Garnier extended family, within the Italian Resistance movement. [72]

The Waldensians have always represented, over the long centuries of their history, an important element of pluralism and of freedom, conserving their faith and their identity in the face of bloody persecution.[73] The Waldensian church is very 'Italian' in its history yet politically and usefully 'foreign' in its way of going about things.

In 2015, Pope Francis visited the Waldensian church in Turin. It was here that many Waldensians endured brutal persecution by the Catholic Church during the Middle Ages. On behalf of the Church, Pope Francis asked Waldensian believers for forgiveness for the persecutions to which Waldensians had been victims over the centuries[74]. "On the part of the Catholic Church, I ask your forgiveness, I ask it for the non-Christian and even inhuman attitudes and behaviour that we have shown you. In the name of the Lord Jesus Christ, forgive us!"

The records show four generations of Garnier were born in Bobbio Pellice between about 1730 and 1844.[75] All were named Jean Garnier, corresponding well with the traditional Waldensian naming pattern: A couple's first son was to be named after the infant's paternal grandfather, (with the second named for the maternal grandfather). The three latest Garnier generations all achieved successful careers beyond the Waldensian valleys.

It was in this Waldensian setting that Giovanni Garnier [76] and Fanny Malan, Albert's parents, my great-grandparents, were brought up. Both were from strongly committed Waldensian families.

Born in Bobbio Pellice in 1844, Giovanni was the son of Jean Garnier and Susanne Negrin, peasants. He married Fanny Malan, whose home was in Angrogna. Both had qualified as elementary school teachers, and had served the Waldensian Church; Giovanni mainly in Rome and Fanny in Livorno, a port city on the Ligurian Sea on the western coast of Tuscany. They had four children.[77]

Giovanni Garnier, Albert's father.

Giovanni was an inaugural student at the Waldensian College and then finished his studies at the Scuola Normale, both in Torre Pellice, where in 1862 he obtained a master's degree. His first assignment was at the Waldensian school of Luserna San Giovanni, then he was called to Tuscany in 1863 to teach in Montecastello and in 1864 at the Waldensian school in Florence, where he remained until 1871, when he moved to Rome at the Gould Institute, of which he became director after the death of the founder Emily Gould.

For some years Giovanni edited *The Evangelical Educator*, a publication of the Italian Evangelical Pedagogical Society, developed by the Waldensian Congress that met in Torre Pellice in 1875, and printed by the Gould Institute. As Society vice-president for some time, his speeches, especially at Society meetings were on problems related to the education of boys and girls. According to Albert, the text of his speeches showed he had a strong grasp of the subject. It was at one of the Society meetings that Giovanni Garnier and Fanny Malan met. Two generations later, in 1987, Benjamin Garnier and Vanna Malan, cousins, married.[78]

In February 1882 Giovanni returned to the Waldensian Valleys for health reasons, but already in the autumn of the same year he was sent as master evangelist to the Waldensian community of San Fedele d'Intelvi, located north of Milan.[79]

But the appointment was short-lived, owing to Giovanni's ill-health. The Waldensian Church in 1883 sent the family to Cannes, on the French Riviera, where Giovanni continued his work as an evangelist and lecturer. He died in Cannes on 22 December 1886, aged 42 and when Albert was four.

One of the few memories Albert had of his father was from Cannes. "I recall vividly my father, pacing up and down on the carpet in the bedroom, trying to teach me to walk properly. The chief trouble with me at the time was a weakness in my ankles." Because of his mother's illness, she had not been able to feed Albert herself and had sent him to a wet nurse in Castel Gandolfo, near Rome. "Here I must have been neglected because, when my mother's sister, Catherine, was called to help the family and fetch me back to Rome to join the others on the way to Cannes, she was alarmed at my appearance."

Fanny and children returned to Angrogna, and a house known as *La Fournasa* because it had been a small brick factory in the remote past. This house, with three rooms downstairs and two upstairs, was where Albert lived for the next 15 years.

Chapter 7:   ALBERT'S LIFE-LONG FAITH AND DOUBTS

FROM an early age, Albert was gripped by an ingrained belief he must lead a life based on 'obedience to the laws of God'.

He had little choice. His parents were devoted Waldensians, and he was descended from a long line of deeply religious devotees. When at age four his father Giovanni died of pneumonia, leaving his mother, Fanny, grieving and impoverished, Albert naturally surrendered to God as 'the standard of all truth, the source of all life, the goal of all endeavour,' as he later put it. Yet for years, he struggled with the inconsistencies between truth and fiction, and what people said and did.

In Cannes, around the time his father died, Albert recalled his fear when a boy took a brush out of his pocket, and, wetting it in his mouth began to rub an ornamental pillar of a balustrade saying: 'I am painting this pillar.' "I waited anxiously to see the ground open beneath his feet and swallow him up! Yet I was not brought up in a religion of fear." Years later, Albert came to understand that, as he put it, "truth can be expressed in fiction".

Answering questions for candidates for mission service in 1906, he said it was "easy" for him to recall the moment when he became sure of his conversion. "At a watch night service in the Baptist Church of Turin, I experienced with unmistakable certainty that I was safe in Christ. A very present consciousness of deep security filled me for a few days; this was followed by a newness of life which has not left me since." [80]

As he grew up in Torre Pellice, Albert admired the Waldensian martyrs for their deeds to ensure the community's survival and the inspiration it provided for his own deep belief in the Kingdom of God. In conversations and writings throughout his life he praises the actions of Waldensian pioneers for their battles against all forms of wrong in the human heart and of oppression among mankind.

Albert believed that justice and righteousness, mercy and peace among men were to be the outcome of a "right relationship to God".

But he was 'worried' by many problems difficult to openly discuss. One of the questions that troubled him early on was that of sin.

"I knew well enough that I was a sinner needing forgiveness, but I knew it through inner conviction which seemed at war with my reason, and I felt that this 'reason' was as much part of me as that 'conviction.'"

He would argue within himself, trying to harmonise conviction with reason, a difficulty increased by his idea of God. "My very mental make-up led me to think of God as being behind everything, and ultimately responsible for everything, including what men regarded as individual freedom.

"If there is an eternal hell, would I say, *'then this hell must be within the ultimate purpose of God, or else there must be another God behind both the 'heaven' and 'hell' of Christian theology.'* Yet all the while my moral sense could not admit of evil in God, and I could not get out of this dilemma.

"I could not divide myself, so to speak, in two halves, the one upholding one thing, and the other believing something else. Somehow, I thought, the two must be united into one whole. Conviction and reason must agree. But how?"

Albert's solution came with help from Italian Nobel Prize winner in Literature, Giosue Carducci's lines: *'Meglio oprando obliar, senza indargarlo – Questo enorme mister de l'universo'* (It is far better, in action, to forget, without probing into it – This enormous mystery of the universe).[81]

"That was it. Mere thinking leads nowhere. After all, a man's reason is not the whole of him. The riddle of the world cannot be solved by thinking alone. A man's thinking is determined largely by the sort of brain he has been endowed with."

He would imagine "a renovated humanity, endowed with power to see reality as it is, able to express, it may be without the form of words, things that are only dimly perceived at present."

"Action was what was expected of a man, not sterile thinking; and I would try to forget speculative problems and work hard. Even now," at age 65, "I am not shocked at any 'heresy' that arises from a thoughtful mind. The conviction has never left me, moreover, that in this world there are two classes of people: those who struggle intellectually and those who don't."

Despite Albert's high thoughts, he harboured, as he put it himself, "a mean spirit on many things." As an adult, he recalled his time in the Waldensian College school battalion 40 years previously that – with uniform of its own, and with real rifles and bayonets – he had never been so proud as when he beat a fellow fifth-form student to be appointed a non-commissioned officer. "Every Saturday afternoon our 'battalion' would muster in the College grounds and we would march through Torre Pellice with drums beating and brass instruments playing."

Albert's early days were hard. Without a father, his mother, Fanny, was virtually the sole authority (other than God) in his life. She was the youngest daughter of a large Waldensian Malan family. Fanny's father, 'Barba Paul Malan,' lived with them till he died; four Garnier children (two daughters, Albert and younger brother Emile) in the small, three-roomed house, *Fournasa* (brick kiln), that Daniel Malan had bought during the French revolution. At this time *Fournasa* had a large farm with it. Daniel's son, Paul Malan, inherited the house and Fanny Garnier took ownership after he died.[82]

Albert claimed he wasn't a good boy, and he was stubborn. He recalled that when seven or eight, the weather turned suddenly very cold just as it was time to break up and go home from school at four o'clock. Dark clouds gathered and the teacher told everyone to go home without stopping, lest those who lived some distance away should be caught in a snowstorm. Had she said nothing, Albert recalled, he would probably have gone straight home, but as it was, "out of sheer cussedness, I loafed about, shying stones at other boys".

Presently the snow began to fall, sparingly at first, then so thickly that Albert could hardly see ten yards, and he began to have a curious feeling in his fingers. "They seemed to swell and to become so numb that, when I tried to put my hands in my pockets for warmth, I realized I couldn't. My hands seemed to have vanished altogether! Filled with terror I began to cry in the middle of the street."

A lady saw him from her upstairs window and came to his rescue. She took him into her house, wrapped up his frozen hands, sat him in front of a fire and gave him a glass of 'vin cuit'.[83] "She was a Roman Catholic. I can still see her kindly face filled with pity under her little lace cap. I still remember how grateful I felt to her, someone who had never seen me before."

Winter illness in the young family was common. The three-year-old Emile had whooping-cough very badly. Albert became dangerously ill with bronchitis. In 1888, the winter was very cold, and eight-year-old Marguerite became ill and died in the room where the family slept. Six feet of snow fell in Torre Pellice; the snow was so deep that only the coffin-bearers could go up to the cemetery beside the Angrogna church. Albert recalls standing outside in the street, trying to look over the sides of the trench, less than two feet wide, cut into the snow to allow people to go to town.

But Fanny was clearly resilient, tough-minded and a caring mother.[84] The three surviving children, Henrietta, Albert and Emile, were all top students of their respective classes at Torre Pellice schools and colleges. She used insurance money she had received to add six new rooms on to the older building so that she might let them to summer visitors. During the rest of the year, she took in as boarders the boys who attended the college, at the foot of the Angrogna Valley, whose homes were too far away for daily travel back and forth to school. She was prepared to house and feed them and supervise their studies, earning enough to keep her children and herself.

Emile gained a degree in Engineering at Turin University, but he refused to support Fascism and was out of work for some years, and during World War II joined the Resistance movement.[85] After the fall of Mussolini, he joined the publishing house of Hoepli in Milan, where he became Scientific Editor of *Sapere*, one of the leading journals in Italy after World War II. Emile also wrote a book on Mathematics which became a long-standing basic text in French and Italian schools.[86]

Henrietta left home at 18 to be a governess to a family in Germany. She travelled widely with various employers, including to China, and spent several years in England. She taught herself to play the piano, and even in her old age could still accompany herself on her mandolin and sing songs in French, Italian, German and English, as well as speak those languages fluently. Like Fanny, she was a dramatic story-teller.

Albert's progress at school was less clear cut. He mentioned his mother's response to his stubbornness: "My mother did not know what to do with me! Once she shut me up in a room where I remained alone all day." In the end, his mother decided to keep Albert away from school for about a year. Fanny gave him some mathematical problems to begin the day, followed by some geography, history and other subjects.

But the 'year of punishment' wasn't all bad. Albert was allowed to go for walks, and learned to love flowers, birds and other features of country life and nature: the feel of the dew, the changing colour of the grass, the blazing heat of summer, the first snows of winter on the high peaks. In the summer Albert and Emile worked on the farms where their cousins were brought up.

While in upper school they would go for long hikes in the Alps. They started two hours before daylight, taking with them a little food, maps, 'and such coppers as we could gather'; and wander about the mountains for three or four days at a time, sleeping wherever they could.

"Even now I feel the fresh air blowing down from the high Alpine passes; I realise the eagerness of making for the mountain top; I recall the grandeur of the sight that met us there; the tired contentment as we followed the trail towards the lowlands in the evening."

In his teenage years, Albert acquired a library of books detailing the deeds of his Waldensian military heroes, and which were marked-up showing the areas of battles won and lost.

Albert would dream, as they tramped along, about "our Waldensian fathers, imagining the great figures of captains Janavel and Jahier rising dark against the frosty ridge of the 'Grand Truc' (in the Cottian Alps), as a challenge to be worthy.

"And as we walked back home along the trail by the Angrogna River the sound of the waters was to me the song of the old Waldensians about whom Professor Jean Jalla used to write and speak." [87] Of Joshua Janavel and Barthelemy Jahier, heroes of the Glorious Return and other battles in the mid-1650s, referred to earlier.

Sometimes Albert and Emile lost their way or got into trouble over some difficult climb. He recounted a three-day and two-night 'walk' with Emile from their house in Angrogna over the Alps into France to see an aunt, travelling almost all the way on foot, with almost no food.

In this way, they visited almost every corner of the Waldensian Valleys, as well as the valleys on the French side of the Alps in that region.

Albert mentioned well into his 60s, still hearing the wind blowing through the pine trees, and seeing the wonderful ranges of mountains stretching far away on every side, with the blue plain beyond, towards the East, recalling the delight and rapture of it all, and his tiredness in the evening.

Albert entered the College in Torre Pellice as top boy of the district and continued to do very well until his last examination when he was just 18. In his own account of his youth, he mentions his dejection at this period and which reinforces his stubborn personality. He felt himself to be overprivileged in receiving his good education, while his cousins on their farms were, in his opinion, just as deserving and intelligent as he. So strongly did this idea seize hold of him, that at the oral examination he remained silent before every question, and do what they could the examiners were not able to induce him to utter a word, although they tried hard, knowing he was one of the ablest students in the area.

So, he failed to qualify for university and, after the summer he went to work in a lace-factory just outside Turin. His work was to wrap up parcels, and his wage was 40 lire a month, soon after transferring to a department drawing patterns for lace making.

This is a classic illustration of what made Albert 'tick' – a deep sense of natural justice and a rejection of self-advancement at the expense of others.

For Albert, the existence of God, the Creator, appears to be a 'given', reinforced by the quasi-mystical personal experience, when he decided to become a missionary. It could be suggested that Albert's view of God as his father is almost as a father substitute, given the loss of his own biological father when he was very young?

His conception of hell lacks evidence, but he loved Dante above all writings except the Bible, and would quote large chunks of his *Inferno*, so may have internalized much of Dante's vision.[88]

Albert clearly saw himself as heir to a very proud and noble league of Waldensian believers who accepted martyrdom as part of the cost of their faithfulness to the 'truth'. He seems to have bought into the comparisons made between Waldensians and Jews,[89] as a despised and persecuted minority with a deep sense of their own history and attachment to a semi-sacred 'homeland'.

But Albert saved himself – just. On the last day of 1900 came a turning point in Albert's life. In Turin, he attended the special Baptist 'new-year's eve' church service, with a former school friend. They came out 'converted and determined' to take up evangelistic work. It was suggested that Albert should proceed to Harley College in London, to train as a Baptist missionary. "For some reason that I couldn't explain, even at that early time, I looked upon China as the field to which I should go."

Too young to go to Harley immediately, he spent part of 1902 at home learning English through reading English books and translating into Italian and French. He spent four years at Harley, where he was 'adopted' by Scottish fellow students – "foreigners in England", they said.

On October the 16th 1906, he left London for Genoa, where he joined the German ship 'Prince Rupert Lintgold' bound for Shanghai and a new life, a missionary and a 'foreign devil' as some saw him.

Thirty-three years later, Albert's youngest son, Beniamino Giovanni Garnier (Benjamin John Garnier) and bride would embark on a sea journey that took him south of Shanghai, to New Zealand, and a New World.

A youthful Ben knew little of Albert's life in China, nor of Albert's passion for Dante, his Waldensian history and the deeds of his military heroes. Ben's youth had been spent in boarding school, successfully playing cricket, rugby and winning a scholarship to Cambridge University. Having 'discovered' a world of science, he had no need for God's love, but he shared with Albert a preparedness to uproot and travel to a remote corner of the world to make a new life independently of the Garnier family and its long-time traditional home in Torre Pellice.

Forty years would go by before Ben would venture to the Val Pellice to live, and fully understand the significance of the feeling of, at last, finally, 'coming home'.

Chapter 8:   SEARCHING FOR FATHER

BORN in China, an Italian national, schooled in Britain, worked in New Zealand, Nigeria, United States and Canada, retired to Torre Pellice, but who was Ben Garnier?

When Ben was born in 1917, a nurse laid him on the top of a chest-of-drawers and he nearly wriggled himself off while her back was turned, which made her declare that he would travel far in life. This he did, both professionally and geographically.

Beniamino Giovanni Garnier (the name Ben used in March 1939 when at age 22 he applied for British citizenship) was, unlike his father, no practicing Waldensian with a love of God. But he had Garnier family Waldensian-like values, a love of freedom, a libertarian, a lover of books, ideas, and music, a committed scholar, a good listener and someone who can get things done. He invariably left individuals in command of their own fate, was enthusiastic and fun to be with.

And yet he communicated a sense of someone who had run away from the religious-led life practiced by his family, but was strongly committed to action to better understand planet Earth. He spent 40 years exploring ideas and initiatives showing how global climate and weather patterns work, change and relate to wider fields – scientific, social and economic. Ben sought in his last 20 years to put mankind's questionable treatment of Earth into a 'scientific' global context, and understand WHY and WHAT could or should be done about it.

Like his father, Ben read widely, thought deeply and wrote up his notes. Ben believed in the possibility of finding the truth concerning solutions to problems of our troubled world. Thus, he could *learn*, he could *grow* in knowledge, even if he can never *know* – that is, know for certain. Ben's citizenship went from the old world to the new – from Italian to British, then New Zealand and Canadian.

The fact that God – or any other authority – commands a person to do a certain thing is no guarantee that the command is *right*. It is "I" who must decide whether to accept the standards of any authority as (morally) good or bad. It is a problem created by people, which people must necessarily solve.

If there is anything 'good' in this approach, Ben said in a last conversation, it is that young people are beginning to understand WHAT is really happening. "My quest is the WHY," he added.

In June 1939, with a new wife (the first of three) and Master of Arts Degree in Geography with Mathematics from St. Catherine's College, Cambridge University, the 22-year-old Ben – three years younger than Albert, when he set sail for China – and Rocky Garnier departed Southampton for far-away New Zealand and a guaranteed teaching position at Wellington Technical College (Rongotai). But World War II broke out while they were at sea, and on arrival Ben was proclaimed to be a Reserve Occupationalist, through his Italian family links, and retained on the bleak Soames Island in Wellington Harbour. This was about the same time that Albert was taken in to internment in England, but for Ben it was a short stay in custody.

Armed with a recommendation letter from the NZ High Commissioner in London, Sir William Jorden, that Ben had a degree and could milk a cow – "which was perfectly true" Ben recalled – Rongotai College appealed and he was quickly released to become the school's geography teacher.

The ambitious Ben's first career jump occurred soon after. He left Rongotai on secondment to the New Zealand Education Department, to prepare a report recommending that geography become a standard subject in New Zealand secondary schools.[90] The same year, 1944, he and Ken Cumberland (also a recent migrant from England, and a geography lecturer at Canterbury University)[91] met in a Wellington hotel bar and over a beer or two, formed the New Zealand Geographical Society and a magazine, *The New Zealand Geographer,* to promote and stimulate the study of geography. The magazine was soon seen as a quality outlet for geographical research, and has earned a high reputation not only in New Zealand, but throughout the world.[92] Ben served as the Society's foundation secretary-treasurer, and in 1952 he became the Society's first life member.

Benjamin Garnier, 1946.

In 1946, Ben was appointed to set up the Geography Department at Otago University, Dunedin, and again, he didn't stay long. In 1951, despite now a family with three children, he moved to Nigeria to establish a geography department at Ibadan University. His time at Ibadan clarified his research and writing ideas, which in 1961 resulted in him heading to Indiana State University in the United States, and membership of an international tropical climate committee, and another move a short time later.

In 1965, Ben was appointed to McGill University in Montreal, Canada, where he stayed nearly 20-years before retiring as Emeritus Professor in 1982. He moved with (third) wife, Vanna, to Torre Pellice and a quiet, satisfying 28-years of retirement with daily walks in the Val Pellice hills and continued his thinking and writing on leading topics of the day.

Between Dunedin, New Zealand, and Torre Pellice, Italy, Ben created a distinguished, knowledgeable and successful 40-year university career legacy in tropical climate. This included completing in 1992 a compendium of notes in climatology for the World Meteorological Organization (WMO), in which he concluded that there "is little doubt" that the increase in carbon dioxide (CO_2) affecting climate conditions must be due to human activity.[93] His personal life led to intensive public speculation, and for Ben, in later life, deep soul searching.

That is the shortened story of Ben, but doesn't answer the question: Who was Ben Garnier?

Born in Tsinan, Shantung in northern China, in 1917, he was 'shipped' to England in 1925, aged eight, to Eltham College, a boarding school for the sons of missionaries, where he had a full and active life. He participated in school plays, was in the 1st XV Rugby team, captained the Cricket 1st XI for three years, 1934-1936, and is described as 'one of the best' slow bowlers the school had ever had.[94] He was head boy in his last year and played cricket in the Middlesex Schools Boys XI. He won a choral scholarship to study at Cambridge University, for he had a fine voice and was, like many in his family, very musical.

An anecdote from Ben's older brother, Wallie, to his son Michael, concerned the school organising a festival cricket match between the boys and a collection of illustrious guest players, including one of England's finest ever batsmen, Jack Hobbs. Ben's mother, Jessie, arrived at the school a little after play had begun and was greeted by a furious headmaster, who told her how angry he was with her son. Knowing Ben, Jessie feared the worst, only to discover that her son's 'crime' had been to dismiss Jack Hobbs, the star attraction whom most people had come to watch bat, very cheaply![95]

Ben met Rocky in 1938 on the Channel Island of Sark. As a Cambridge student he had to write an original essay as part of his degree. The essay was about land use in Sark. "I knew some people who ran a café, and asked if I could be a waiter for the summer. Then one day I saw this girl coming off the boat. Rocky was visiting. Then we married and decided to emigrate."[96]

Of the Cambridge graduate students in Ben's year (1938/39), no one got a job in England. "I didn't think of the armed forces, and said I would go where I was employable – and that turned out to be New Zealand." He was offered a job in Australia after graduating, but the New Zealand High Commissioner, Sir William Jorden, persuaded him to come to New Zealand, and provided a letter of recommendation, Ben recalled. An assisted passage for the sea voyage was part of the inducement.

After five years in Wellington, he moved to Dunedin to establish Otago University's Department of Geography. It was only after Ben was appointed that a full degree programme in geography was offered to undergraduate students.[97]

The first lecture in the Otago geography programme was scheduled for a March afternoon in 1946. The venue was Mellor House, which had been a family home, and was used by the University as a residence for male students. Accommodation was found for the fledgling department by combining two ground floor rooms into a lecture room, next to which was a staff office in what had been the pantry off the kitchen. The rooms lacked furniture although the 'office' had a built-in sink. Right from the start it was a simple matter to establish what was to become the departmental tradition of tea and coffee breaks! A 'Garnier Room' was established and formalized decades later when the university precinct was modernized.

On the morning of the first day of classes, with the students scheduled to assemble at 4pm, only a blackboard and a low platform for the lecturer were in place. Soon after lunch, to Ben's relief, a van arrived with tables and chairs, and all was made ready for the first lecture. But when Ben entered the lecture room, he could hardly believe his eyes. Every seat was taken. Some students were seated at the tables, others were leaning against the walls, and a substantial number had to stand on the verandah outside the lecture room. Rather than 20 to 25 students he had been advised to expect, between 70 and 80 undergraduates had decided to study geography. Ben's planned lecture had to be rescheduled – but he took the opportunity to welcome the students, speak about the course, and express pleasure at seeing so many people – until he could find a larger room for the class.

Field trips, articles and books quickly followed, all focusing on the importance of geography for understanding the economic and social development potential of Otago and New Zealand.

In 1948, as part of the Otago centennial celebrations, Ben proposed and edited a book titled *The Face of Otago* and contributed chapters on the climate of Otago. The book provided a record of 100 years of 'human habitation' in the province,[98] and predicted that the future prosperity of Central Otago in particular lay in the soil and climate "which can be utilized to great advantage, provided the concept of land exploitation is replaced by that of land husbandry". [99] Few would have anticipated that within 50 years, the prediction of the area becoming a popular location for the production of grapes[100] would translate into one of the world's top-quality wine-producing areas and a flourishing tourism centre.

Similarly, the Foreword to *New Zealand Weather and Climate*, published in 1950, highlighted the growth in the importance of weather forecasting. Without this kind of vehicle for responding to the persistent demand for information on New Zealand weather and climate, the information would exist "only in a typed and cardboard-bound volume on the shelf of a university library." Again, the rise of the climate crisis reinforced the perceptiveness of Ben in 1950 bringing the volume together, including climatic data for 40 stations in New Zealand.

The work that Ben was best known for outside New Zealand in his early career was *The Climate of New Zealand*, which was published in 1958. Despite New Zealand being a small land mass surrounded by a hemisphere consisting almost entirely of ocean,[101] the climate displays considerable diversity – "it is a vigorous climate, containing sunshine and storms, fine weather and heavy rain, stimulating air and sudden change". The book is the first account showing the essential link between climate and detailed landforms, growth of vegetation, and erosion. Nine climatic regions are described in detail for the first time, "in the hope that this may be of some practical value". [102]

When Ben moved to Ibadan University, Nigeria, in 1951, he undertook a similar pioneering mission to that at Otago University. He started and developed the Honours School in Geography, and also took part in the development of geography teaching in schools, through his work with the Nigerian Geographical Association of which he was president.

In both New Zealand and Nigeria, his field of research was climatology, with special emphasis in Nigeria on the heat and moisture balance and problems of heat in the tropics.

In Ibadan, he was Professor of Geography, and for a time Dean of the Faculty of Arts. He was quickly recognized as a specialist in tropical climatology and was appointed to the Humid Tropics Commission of the International Geographical Union, a body that he served with distinction for 10 years.

While in Nigeria, Ben set up an evaporation research station. A device he developed for measuring evapotranspiration became well known around the world. He also contributed significantly (with Atsumu Ohmura) on modelling solar irradiance on slopes; their work was a landmark in that field and became highly relevant to the solar energy industry.[103]

Ben's research found that the Thornthwaite formula for computing potential evapotranspiration would not provide realistic values under the conditions of Nigeria – greatly varying atmospheric moisture and generally unvarying temperature. Ben developed correction factors to modify the computed values of potential evapotranspiration for tropical savanna climates.[104]

He soon moved on from Nigeria – to Bloomington, Indiana in the United States. And after just four years at the University of Indiana between 1961 and 1965, working with Professor Kimble as a member of the Tropics Commission of the International Geographical Union, Ben came to McGill. He replaced Ken Hare as head of the geography department. He was attracted by the unique opportunities for field studies. McGill maintained weather stations and field studies in climatology on Axel Heiberg Island, at Knob Lake (Schefferville), in Montreal, on Barbados and in British Guiana.

In particular, the Bellairs Research Institute in Barbados became the headquarters for Ben and a group of faculty and graduate students working in tropical agricultural climatology and the variations of solar radiation at the surface of the earth.

Shortly after arriving at McGill, Ben fulfilled a plan to produce a new journal of climatology. Known as the *Climatological Bulletin*, Ben edited and published issues twice-yearly, introducing new programmes and invigorating ideas on the distribution and role of solar radiation at the surface of the earth, and in applied climatology, especially in its relation to atmospheric pollution. In the 1970s, the magazine gained a big circulation and influence beyond McGill.[105]

Ben's combined teaching and research involved frequent trips between Montreal and Barbados. A project on maritime microclimatology for the United States Navy resulted in some activist students black-listing Ben for receiving military money, despite the fact that the research into radiation balances is open book science. Ben: "I felt rather proud; it's the first time anyone has given my modest efforts any publicity."[106]

As Chair of the geography department, Ben acted with "tact, skill and good humour". His quiet manner won him many battles before they even became battles.[107]

Ben gave students free rein in developing their climatological research interests, and always left individuals in command of their own fate. A student who gave Ben a rough draft of his MSc received the following response: "I will reread it and comment upon it as often as you care to hand it to me, but the decision, my friend, as to when to submit it is yours."

Another student who Ben found particularly noteworthy informed him some years later: "When I think back on our time, I realize that what you gave me is hope. This is not the easy hope to obtain a degree or a position but a true hope to pursue a scientific destiny to which one's mind is taken. ... I have often asked myself what the essence of an education could be; to transfer a knowledge and experience from one generation to the next as efficiently as possible? And many other answers could be possible. And in these problem-filled times, I am convinced that at least one of the most important qualities of education is to give a true hope to young people. You already gave me just that."

Following his retirement in 1982, Ben continued to work on a variety of projects, including a revised 1970 compendium of lecture notes in climatology for the World Meteorological Organization (WMO).[108] Published in 1992, the purpose of the updated compendium is to provide a basic understanding of climatology and its applications for training personnel involved in operational climatology. The principles of climate, regional and local variations, and climate change are covered together with climatic applications, data observation, analysis and the scientific framework within which operational climatology lies. The 1992 compendium clearly linked climate change with growth of world population.

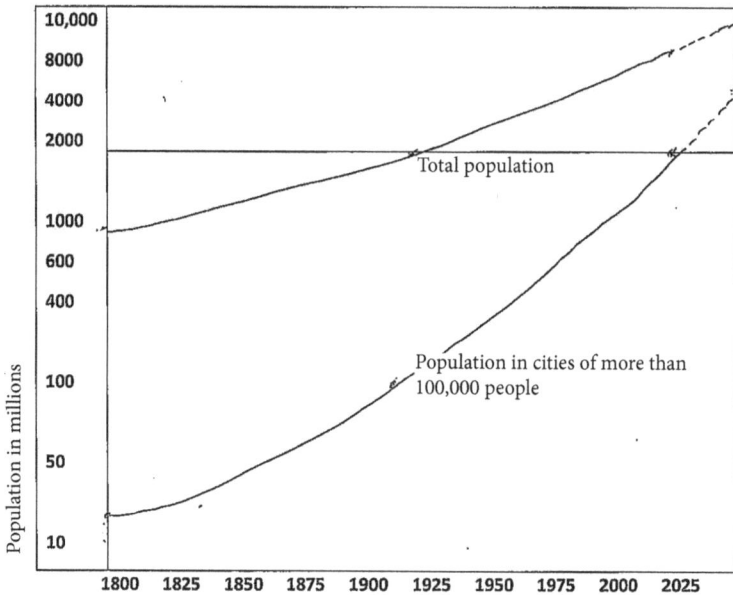

Growth of world population since 1800. Note: The vertical scale is a logarithmic scale. Source: WMO-726, p.54.

Drawing on evidence from many parts of the world, the core of Ben's case is that carbon dioxide (CO_2) in the atmosphere has risen from an estimated 280 parts per million by volume (ppmv) in 1850 to 330 ppmv or more by 1970 and that this is a continuing trend solely attributable to human influence.[109]

Ben's conclusion: "There is little doubt that this increase is due to human activity."

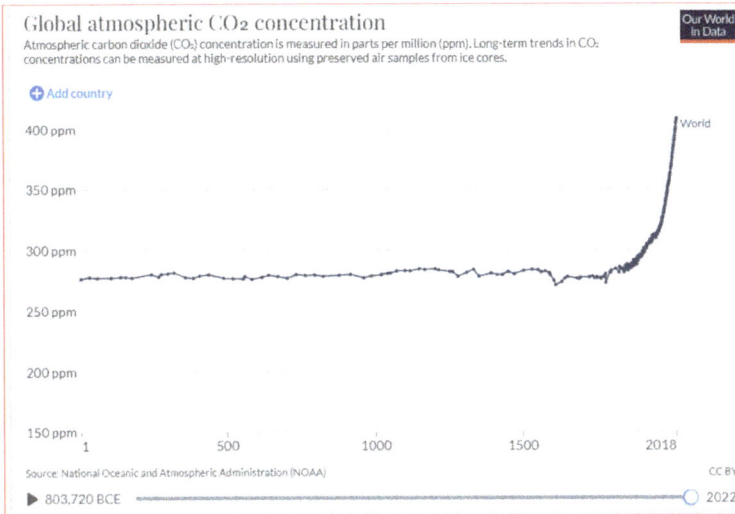

Increases in atmospheric carbon dioxide (CO_2) concentrations from BC to 2020. Ben's conclusion: "There is little doubt that this increase is due to human activity." Source: WMO.

He has been proved to be correct. The rise in atmospheric carbon dioxide (CO_2) concentrations continues and is becoming more dramatic. By mid-July 2020, CO_2 values had reached between 385 ppm and 405 ppm in the atmosphere. By May 2022, they had reached 420.99 ppm, an increase of nearly 2ppm over 2021.[110]

There has been a lot of talk on the need for action, but no sign yet of CO_2 values starting to reduce to below 250ppm, where they were in the pre-industrial world.

Ben: "The natural environment maintains a fairly steady level of CO_2 in the atmosphere by the normal processes of growth and decay in vegetation, bacteria and living organisms generally. There has been no reason for any noticeable change in these general, environmentally produced background processes during the past century. The observed increase in CO_2 must therefore be due to human activity."

He noted that the most obvious human activity and source of atmospheric carbon dioxide is from burning of fossil fuels, which has increased enormously since 1900. An equally important factor has been a change in land use: deforestation and agricultural expansion have drastically reduced the overall quantity of biomass in the world. Accordingly, CO_2 has been released into the atmosphere in quantities that are comparable with the amount produced by the burning of fossil fuels.

The potential climatic impact of increased CO_2 in the atmosphere will be an overall rise in the global temperature. There is, however, clearly a lot of monitoring and a lot of work for climatologists and others to do in this field. But the best current estimates appear to imply "slight temperature changes in equatorial regions but a noticeably larger change – an increase of perhaps as much as 4°C – in polar regions". Other changes include in precipitation and the length of the growing season.

Ben compiled evidence showing that different forms of change and variability operate at different time scales within the climatic system. He came up with six varying time scales of the fluctuations which occur: From one day to a few weeks; from one month to one year; from one year to 10 years or more; from 10 to 100 years; from 100 to thousands of years; and, millions of years.[111]

Under the *millions of years* time scale, he noted that fossil and paleoclimatic records point to catastrophic changes approximately every 25-30 million years which are involved with the mass extinction of entire species on Earth. "For example, the dinosaurs which existed over 100 million years (mankind has thus far managed a mere 5 million years) were rather abruptly terminated. Fluctuations at this time scale are rather difficult to grasp mentally. It is easy to assume we do not need to be concerned about them. It would, however, be nice to be sure about this. It would be most uncomfortable to be frozen while eating dinner – purportedly what happened to mammoths in the Siberian area!"

With regard to the world's slow effort to get nations to limit warming to 1.5°C above pre-industrial levels,[112] it is significant that the estimated change in average global temperature between non-glacial and glacial times is only about 10°C over the past 100 million years. Small variations may well produce significant changes in the global distribution of snow and ice or in precipitation and weather conditions, with particular effect in climatically sensitive or transitional areas.[113]

The point: if humanity is the primary agent in the sharp rise in carbon dioxide, it is now time to realize that like a government with a perennial hundred-billion-dollar deficit or thinking of using nuclear weapons to solve a territorial dispute, we are in a situation in which we can no longer allow carbon dioxide continuing to rise indefinitely, or allow runaway inflation or a nuclear winter to occur.

Ben's primary work and thinking was not yet done. With the lack of focus by world leaders to action an agreed solution on CO_2, he began to question the capability of mankind to cope with designing clear strategies to solve other problems with global impacts – population increase, nuclear warfare, and deforestation. How do we cope? Do those leading the global initiative on climate change underway fully understand the scale of the problem mankind faces?

He would work out an answer: the solution to the riddles of the world depends on expanding the brain's powers of learning and reasoning. It is only a question of time before these global issues are addressed, he believed, thanks to the rapid evolution of the brain's unlimited reasoning powers. The question is whether the continuing evolution of the brain's learning and reasoning capacity is fast enough to enable mankind to organize the global action required for survival.

There is no other way if mankind is not to become the sixth extinction – we must collectively evolve better ways to use our brains

Ben suggests how this might be achieved, in Chapters 10 and 12 below.

Ben's family complications …

When Ben moved to Nigeria in 1950, contact was lost with wife Rocky and his three New Zealand children, until well after he moved to Canada in 1965. In 1970 an exchange of letters with three of his four children began, by then all were adults. But often there was a long break, then a letter would arrive in which Ben exclaimed that it must be two years since he last wrote: "I seem to have the characteristic that the very persons I love and think about most are the ones I am slow in maintaining contact with, probably because I am impelled by feeling rather than by any sense of duty." [114]

Finally, in mid-1975 in response to my letter suggesting that my wife Juliet and I visit him in Montreal, Ben offers a comfortable couch or overflow to a carpeted floor. But makes it clear: "I'm excited at the prospect of seeing you."

A couple of months later, before our visit, he writes admitting that he has been doing some major soul searching involving some pricy counselling. "I now see that there was no real need for Rocky and I to break up so completely and much of it was due to my intransigence and weakness. I bitterly regret the part I played but it took me many years to see this. When I did there was no chance of unwinding my foolishness." He suggested a longer visit than a week: "We could get to know each other better and perhaps this would do something to make up for the past 25 years and help you toward a future without regrets."

On meeting Ben in 1976 in Montreal, and where his turbulent personal relationships began to emerge into full view, but with humour, wine and pasta we quickly embrace – our souls are in repair. Three short letters quickly follow our visit as we track back to New Zealand: "Your visit seemed dreamlike – until I got your welcome postcard from New York as tangible evidence of your presence in North America."

Journalism takes me to Ottawa a year later, a surprise for Ben and tagged with plans for further visits to Montreal and Italy (where we hope to meet up). "I watched your plane until it was a spot in the sky when you left from Ottawa. But this time I didn't feel nearly so desolate as when you left a year ago. I'll be seeing you again soon and, also, I feel we know each other now – I have an adult face to see in my mind, a voice to hear in my head instead of just imaginings. Soon it will be the same in respect of Susan and Christopher – and for them too."

Later that year, Ben mentions my courage and determination to visit Montreal, followed by our next visit, which broke the ice and allowed him to visit New Zealand. "But for these visits I would still be wallowing in my ignorance and misconception of all that I now know."

A lot changed for Ben. Accounts of his separation from Rocky, and his second marriage in Nigeria, to English lecturer and poet Joyce Green, are gradually pieced together. It suggests a somewhat complicated personal life, until Ben eventually found peace in the relationship with and marriage to Vanna, a cousin, in 1978.

In August 1951, Rocky and the children had packed up their Dunedin home and travelled to Wellington ready to take a ship to Genoa, Italy, where they would be met by a relative and escorted to England. But we never caught the ship. A telegram was received, telling Rocky not to travel and that it would be best to seek a divorce. Rocky had a break-down and Christopher and I were sent to Cathedral Grammar School in Christchurch for two terms.

But Ben insisted (in 1975): "I didn't send a telegram. It wasn't the intention. The intention was that you should go to England while I was in Nigeria. ... I don't think she intended to divorce me, but the solicitors more or less advised her to. I remember when I was in Ibadan, I got the news that you were all staying in New Zealand – I burst into tears."

Who sent the telegram is unclear. The solicitors? I asked Ben: Did

Enrica (Ben's sister) have something to do with it? She had visited NZ at the time and was recovering from a broken relationship.[115] Ben: "Yes – she poked her nose in. Enrica was a great interferer. Everything was arranged. I had a booking on a ship from Wellington. A friend was going to meet the boat in Genoa and put you on a train to London, but it all just collapsed."

I find it difficult to believe that Enrica would try to end Ben's relationship with his wife and children, and tend to believe the telegram came from the Dunedin-based solicitors. Well-known Dunedin writer Charles Brasch, reported a conversation with poet Basil Dowling in August 1951 who told him that his wife Margaret had decided to leave and go with Ben. "Margaret had gone to Sydney for a month, to meet Ben Garnier" on his way to Nigeria.[116] Margaret will come back to Dunedin, then take her children to England. And Basil will remain in Dunedin.

However, according to Brasch, by March 1952 Basil had resigned from the Otago University library and gone to England "because he feels that not only the children but Margaret may need him, so that he should be near them." [117]

Meanwhile Ben formed a relationship with Joyce Green, a fellow member of the Ibadan University staff. They were married in the late 1950s and had a daughter Stephanie in 1957.

Ben described his marriage to Joyce as a disaster. Ben and Joyce separated in 1961 when Ben moved to the United States of America, and were eventually divorced in the late 1970s.

Between moving from Nigeria to the United States, concerned about the reaction of his parents to his marriage breakups, Ben wrote to his father to see if it was okay to visit. Albert's response was not in words, but a brief letter that included the key to his and mother's, Jessie's, house in Sevenoaks, Kent. The visit went well, Ben recalled.

Through the seventies Ben repaired relationships with his three New Zealand children and met Vanna Stalle, a cousin, who he married in June 1978, and in Ben's words 'never looked back'. Together they visited New Zealand in 1987.

Ben and Vanna had met briefly in Torre Pellice in the 1950s, and again by chance when both were visiting long-settled United States Waldensian/Torre Pellice relatives in Middlesborough, Virginia. The Stalles are related to the Garniers through the female line; Henri Malan, a Angrogna land owner had three daughters:

Fanny who married a Garnier (1882), and is Ben's grandparent

Margerite who married a Stalle, and is Vanna's grandparent
Catherine who married a Forneron.

For Ben, after a life travelling from China, to England, to New Zealand, to Nigeria, to the United States, to Canada, to Val Pellice in northern Italy he was finally home. He wrote in the front of "The Glorious Recovery by the Vaudois (Waldensians) of their Valleys" by Henri Arnaud, in 2009, shortly before he died, in a gift to his great-grandson Oscar, "so that you may learn the history of the valleys where your forefathers lived." Malan, Garnier and Forneron individuals were named by Arnaud as 'heroes of the glorious repatriation' of 1689. Some 320 years later the three families link continues.

Chapter 9: ALBERT'S DESPAIR WITH THE WORLD

From anguish with British justice ....

LONDON: The knock on the door was expected, but not so early. It was 7am on the 14th of June 1940, the day before Albert's 59th birthday. He was shaving and half-dressed.

Four days earlier Italy had entered the war on the side of the Nazis. Albert knew he was likely to be questioned, having visited Italy and his mother in Torre Pellice on his return journey from Shanghai. He had put his papers in order. Yet when the police came, he was surprised and too upset to eat any breakfast as the police officer considerately advised.

The policeman asked to see Albert's passport and Alien Registration Book, and said he must go with him to Bromley Police Station. On the way the police car stopped near the house of another Italian who was to be picked up. He was still in bed, but after a while the detective came back with a fellow-captive, a man of about 40.

At Bromley Police Station they were locked in to a small room to wait for other Italians who were being rounded up. One was weeping quietly, while Albert tried to keep calm by reading a book. After a while another man appeared, a seaman who began at once to crack a number of jokes. He seemed to be concerned about a dog he had left at home.

After an hour or so, a tall gentleman of distinguished appearance was brought into the crowded room. "I was attracted to him at once, for I recognized in him a man of culture, but gave little thought at the time that he and I would become friends and spend practically the whole of our internment together." His name was Danilo Lehrecht, but as Albert soon discovered, he was better known under his nom de plume of Lorenzo Montano, a poet and writer.[118]

Lorenzo Montano.

About 11am the Chief of the Alien Department came in with their passports and informed them that he had no alternative but to send them away for internment. They were put in a Black Maria van to start a journey to an unknown destination, and so began a tumultuous and difficult three months for Albert and Jessie, and his extended family.

Albert's mother had died early in June in Torre Pellice. His younger brother, Emile, a long-standing anti-fascist had joined the Italian Resistance movement, and his mother's Malan family relatives were organizing to resist Germany's entrenchment. As Albert would soon become painfully aware, Torre Pellice was the headquarters of the resistance, as refugees from Turin poured in to escape the air raids.

Jessie and Albert's relatives would hear nothing of Albert's fate for weeks.

As they sped along in the Black Maria, Lorenzo and Albert quickly discovered interests in common. In Italy, Albert had met Bruno Revel,[119] a well-known Italian translator and editor, and they began to talk about books, for Lorenzo Montana represented in England the firm of Montadori who Revel worked for in Milan. It was through Lorenzo that many English books had been translated into Italian and published by Montadori.

"He told me then, and I learned more later, about himself and his family." He was of Jewish origin, but had joined the Roman Catholic Church. His home was in Verona, where the family had resided for many years and where they were well-known and beloved. During the Great War, Lorenzo had been an officer in the Grenadiers, for he was well over six feet tall, reminding Albert of the 'Hussar fidèle' whom Victor Hugo's father loved: *pour sa grande bravoure, et pour sa haute taille*.

Not liking the Fascist regime and also not being free from persecution, Lorenzo had left Italy, and after a time in Switzerland where he had been connected with a Swiss newspaper, he had arrived in England two years earlier. "His wife was English by birth, but, like Jessie, Italian by marriage," Albert recalled.

As they travelled to who knows where, they already felt deeply that the crowds outside in the streets and themselves belonged to two different worlds that had nothing to do with the other.

Shortly after midday they arrived at the Oratory School in Fulham and were handed over to the Military Authorities. Herded into a yard packed with internees and forced to wait, while other batches of arrested men arrived, Albert was bewildered.

"I shall never forget that crowd! All sorts of men were there, old and young, rich and poor, tall and short, fat and thin." It seemed less than fair to be taken from his home, without a chance of saying a word or he or his wife being told what was going to happen to him. "All the time I kept thinking that a mistake had been made, and that presently someone would call for me and send me home. *Sancta simplicitas!*"

It was not to be. During the afternoon, buses began to take away groups of about 30 men at a time. "When our turn came, we were lined up before an officer who called out our names, and then we were marched off to our conveyance by soldiers with fixed bayonets." The bus sped westwards.

That terrible impression of belonging to a new world – entirely removed from the accustomed one – was fast intensifying. "Only a few hours before I had been at home, and 'home' seemed already a dim memory of the past, much more than it had ever seemed during the long separation from my wife and children in China."

Arriving at Kempton Park Race Course, they were searched and personal items were taken, everything – books, papers, money – and put in an envelope with his name. Then an interview process began. A lieutenant poured out on the table the contents of Albert's envelope and saw the Chinese book he had brought with him and read the letters about the Liverpool censorship position. "You ought not to be here," he said, "I know," Albert replied.

He left the book and some blank paper, but kept all the rest, and gave Albert a slip of paper with the number – 558 – and a record of the amount of money impounded, about three pounds.

After a long weary time of waiting, he was led with a dozen others to one of the buildings.

Montano was waiting for him. "The good fellow had managed to secure for me a mattress next to his own." The room was on the ground floor of the race-course building, and was dirty and very dark. The chief trouble by this time, however, was hunger, and there was no sign of a meal.

After a while, somebody shouted that they could get a spoon, a tin plate and a tin mug. They were filthy, but there was plenty of water and using sand in the yard they soon cleaned them up.

It was well after 8pm when food arrived in the yard – Albert's first meal of the day! "How we rushed for it! And how we pushed one another to get some of it! But at last, we managed to have our bowl almost filled with thin soup, and to secure a chunk of bread. That was something and we went to bed on it."

"The next morning Montano and I set out to clean the place. We found some brooms and worked with a will. Our chief difficulty was to find a place to get rid of the rubbish."

But there was still utter disorder with the distribution of food. It was brought into the yard, set on a table, and they lined up to get their share. "When I say 'lined up', I mean rather that we rushed round, pushing one another out of the way."

As for communications with the outside world, there was none. No one received a message during the whole time of their stay. But they could write a brief note of three or four lines. There were no postcards, but fortunately Albert had some note-paper which he used.

They spent their days, wandering about over the grounds and becoming acquainted with one another.

Although forbidden, political discussions were common. What rule can prevent a mass of nearly 1,000 men gathered in one place, from speaking with one another of the various views on why they were interned. "But to the credit of these men, never was there even the beginning of a disturbance in the camp," Albert recalled.

There were distinct sections: first, the Jews who had left Italy for obvious reasons. Most of these were professional men – barristers, doctors, professors and teachers.

In fact, the Grenadier Sergeant-Major in charge – a man known in civilian life to a number of internees as an attendant at the Savoy – wittingly remarked one day that half of our crowd was made up of Jews, and the other half of people who couldn't read! An exaggeration to be sure, but descriptive nevertheless, said Albert.

Then (second and third) they had political or semi-political exiles, and the mass of people who loved both Italy and England and were not identified with any party.

One of the chief points of discussion was the Axis. What was Italy's real position in it? How did Italy expect any advantage from being linked up with Germany? And, on this point, there were very different but firm views.

Those who were acquainted with the history of Italy, who had been brought up, like Albert, on the writers of the Risorgimento Era,[120] could see no good ever coming to Italy from a German-Italy alliance. The opinion was freely expressed that, whoever won the war, Italy had already lost it. Many could not see any hope for their country except in a British victory. The Fascists, of course, vigorously opposed such views, and poured out invective against England which reminded Albert of how the Chinese used to behave during the anti-British agitation in China of 1925-27.

After nearly a fortnight, news came at last that we were to be taken somewhere else, but where, nobody knew. Some said Liverpool, others Devonshire, others Yorkshire, others the Isle of Man.

"Montano and I were beginning to lose hope. Why should we be treated like this? We were still within a few miles of home, and yet the days had passed without our being told what was going to happen to us. We felt it less than fair to be treated like this without a chance of saying a word in our defence."

The idea constantly recurred to Albert that a mistake had been made, and that presently he would be sent home. "But when we were told to be ready to start within an hour, all hope disappeared, and I am afraid I began to doubt the reality of the British justice of which I had so often spoken highly of to the Chinese."

On June 24th they were lined up and marched off with soldiers on either side to the train station at Kempton Park. "As we filed by, some of the Grenadiers amused themselves by kicking in the backsides of some of the internees."

A train was waiting and we were locked in, eight in each compartment, and supplied with a chunk of bread and a piece of cheese – a whole day's journey was ahead. "By this time, we were almost certain that the Isle of Man was our destination."

It was a slow journey, but soon Albert knew they were on the London, Midland and Scottish Line that goes through Kenton. "As we passed that station and the miniature golf course where Ben and I used to play, I felt that life was slipping from me."

"Whatever happened, whoever won or lost this war, whether I would ever return home or not, I knew that something in my conception of life, of human justice, something of my faith in man had gone, never to return. I remember little of that journey, as we sped over the Midlands towards Liverpool."

In the next compartment there was a small man, hardly five feet tall, who seemed very dejected. Montano went to speak to him, then came back and called Albert out into the passage. "Do you know who is there?" he asked. "It is Professor Gaetano Loria, a friend of King George, whom he treated for stuttering." The diminutive, round-faced, plump little man had been received many times by the King. He had letters from him. "I helped him," he said dejectedly, "and this is my reward."

It was dark when they arrived at Liverpool somewhere near the river, and were marched off to a boat moored alongside. "She seemed to me more like Noah's Ark than a boat, and I noticed at once that she was already full." Given a life-belt Albert preferred to stay on deck; "if we struck a mine, or were bombed from the air, I thought I would prefer to be outside than in."

"That night was one of the most dreadful I have ever spent in my life, and to describe it is impossible." Dead tired, faint with hunger and cold, Albert sat on the deck surrounded by a thick mass of fellow-internees, every minute seeming as long as a day. Montano and two colleagues were with him.

Before long Liverpool sirens screeched and all the lights went out. There was a raider overhead – some of the internees vowed they could see it – and there they stood, wondering whether a bomb would drop on them.

After what seemed to Albert an eternity, the "all clear" was given and they started again. How cold it was! Montano had found a corner, inside a partition, where the Scots Fusiliers of the escort had their quarters. "One of them was seasick and looked as miserable as myself, I fancy!"

Montano began a conversation with a kindly corporal and told him Albert had been a Baptist missionary in China. "Out came the good fellow, bringing his ration of bread and bully beef, and a tin of the best hot tea I ever drank! Presently, he brought me more. Then he opened a tin of pineapple and handed it round. Again, as I gratefully drank and ate, the futility of war and the refreshing sense of the brotherhood of man filled me. I felt like cursing nationalities and blessing mankind."

The kindness of this corporal, whose name Albert tried in vain to discover, "is another memory of my internment which will outlast all else."

We arrived at Douglas on the Isle of Man in the morning, and it was no easy task for the 1,700 internees on board to disembark with their luggage.

A walk of about 20 minutes brought them to a block of 31 boarding houses, along the seafront, which had been fenced off. A double row of barbed-wire had been erected about 15 feet away from the front of the houses. "We went through a double gateway of barbed-wire and there we were, like birds in a cage."

No one who has not experienced it can understand the feeling. When they entered the already overcrowded dining room of a house set up for 85 people, some kindly young fellows brought them a cup of tea and a slice of bread and jam. "By my side I noticed a tall, imposing-looking, gentleman who had come in with us and, when we gave our names, he immediately asked me "Are you a Waldensian?" "Yes," I replied. "I thought so by your name. In Glasgow I used to meet some of your people; young ministerial students who had come to Scotland for a post-graduate course in theology." His name was Turcotti, and he had acted as vice-consul in Glasgow.

Isle of Man internment camp for Italians during World War II.

"Presently I and a colleague were assigned a room at the top of the building hoping for some rest. Our joy was short-lived, however, for we found the room already occupied by two sour-looking individuals who at once began to run down England and all her ways! There were only two beds in the place, and the prospect of sharing one with our new companions was by no means enticing. In fact, none of us liked it, but we raided the house and managed to find two dilapidated camp-beds which, with those already there, filled the room completely."

In this way Albert's life in the Isle of Man's Palace Internment Camp began!

From his bedroom window Albert could see a steep slope covered with shrubs and wild flowers that reminded him of home in the Waldensian Valleys. But all that was unreal: between the flowers and him there was a double row of barbed-wire. He now belonged to another world in which beautiful things were only shadows. "The bluer the sky, the brighter the sun, the greener the grass – the more did we feel the wounds that the barbed-wire cut into the flesh of our souls. Never before had freedom seemed such a lovely and distant possession."

Montano had landed in an empty house and been appointed House Leader. He spent the first few days organising the various services of the house, appointing cooks, assigning the members of his large family of 90 or 95 to the various rooms and attending to the numberless details pertaining to his new office.

But this sort of thing did not suit Montano. He was a man of larger ideas and wanted to keep free from administrative details. His deliverance – and Albert's as well – came unexpectedly and soon. As he was walking one day along the narrow parade, he saw an officer whose face seemed familiar. "Hallo Montano," cried the latter, "what in the world are you doing here?" This officer was a Maltese, Lieutenant De Borg, whom Montano had met in civilian life, when both had been connected with the world of books.

De Borg at once took Montano to the Camp Leader, Filippo del Guidice, and introduced him as a personal friend, recommending that Montano be given some position on the Camp Staff – "The Commando" – as internees called it.

Del Guidice was delighted. He was organising the various services in the Camp entrusted to the internees themselves, and needed reliable men to help him, especially as he knew that he himself must be at the disposal of the British Military Authorities.

Montano had a long conversation with him and kindly recommended that Albert, too, be assigned to some general service in the Camp. "I am afraid that he must have sounded my praises rather high, for Del Guidice at once accepted me as one of his helpers, and consistently showed me much respect. In fact, Montano and I became members of a sort of Cabinet, where delicate matters were discussed. Shall I ever forget these little meetings, often held in the dark, after lights out in Del Guidice's office, while he sat at his desk, smoking his inevitable cigar!"

The new position involved a change of house for both Albert and Montano, to "The Commando", next to the hospital. This house was run differently to the rest. Elsewhere the inmates took turns with the house-duties and Camp services, but in "The Commando" these were performed by a group of 30 sailors, leaving the internee's 'Cabinet' free for office and other work.

"A new life was beginning for me. Had it not been for that oppressive feeling of lost freedom, and for the uncertainty about our future, this internment could have been fruitful in lessons that could be learned nowhere else."

Through letter writing Albert undertook for others, he knew how much suffering there was among his fellow-internees. A letter Albert crafted for someone who had openly opposed Mussolini, and yet was treated now as if he were his friend: *"I am a fool,"* he said, with tears in his voice, *"to believe in justice and yet I cannot help it. To me justice and honour are greater things than patriotism; they are more precious than life. I am a child, not fit to live in a world like this."*

And then another letter he wrote was for someone whose admiration for and loyalty to the Duce are complete: *The Duce can do no wrong!*

Albert was appointed Chairman of the Welfare Committee. The function was to co-ordinate the welfare activities in the Camp and to suggest improvements.

"I set to work with a will, urging that various sub-committees be set up to look after the canteen, education, sports, relief, entertainments and workshops." The idea was approved. Each sub-committee was practically independent, but the activities of each were correlated through the Welfare Committee itself.

The education work was a success. Daily lectures were arranged by compelling all our professors and experts into service. Some of the lectures were highly technical, including one on *Blue Coal*, some on the *Bible,* the *rudiments of language, navigation* and many other topics.

Albert spoke on missionary work in China. "I don't think I ever had a more appreciative, intelligent, and I may add, surprised audience. I was peppered with questions afterwards, both after the lecture and on subsequent occasions.

"Most of these men had only the haziest ideas as to what missionary work actually was. They evidently looked upon it as an enterprise of well-meaning cranks, bent on thrusting down the throats of the "heathen" an ancient creed bearing no relation to modern life. They were surprised to hear about schools, universities, hospitals, and the production and distribution of books."

Impact of the *Arandora Star* disaster

In early July, persistent rumours began to circulate that they were to be sent to Canada, but soon stopped when news arrived of the *Arandora Star* disaster that resulted in more than 400 Italian citizens dying. The disaster probably saved Albert and other captives from being shipped to Canada.

The *Arandora Star* was on her way to Canada with 1,560 Italian 'prisoners', many from Scotland – shop owners, barbers, market salesmen – who had been arrested by the British as they were considered a threat, just like Albert and colleagues from London, when Italy had allied with Germany. The ship was also carrying 400 troops to guard the prisoners and some heavy machine guns for protection. Then on 1st July, a German U-boat spotted the *Arandora Star* and sank her with a single torpedo. The Italians began clambering into the lifeboats to save themselves from drowning but the British shot holes in the lifeboats to stop them from escaping. 682 people perished including 200 soldiers. The surviving Italians were shipped back to Liverpool where they were transported to prison camps in Australia the following week.[121]

When news of the sinking of the *Arandora Star* began to filter through there was consternation in the Camp. Stories were told about the German internees on the boat fighting down their Italian fellow-captives, to be saved first. "Many of our people feared that relatives or friends were among the drowned," Albert recalled.

Camp leader Del Giudice was given a list of casualties, and asked to inform relatives with necessary tact. He did not like the job for he feared distressing scenes, and even some disorder. He called together all the clergymen in the Camp and they agreed to his suggestion that the relatives of the survivors be informed at once, and that the others be told of the loss on the following day. This latter task was entrusted to the Roman Catholic clergyman, Padre Negrini.

It was a sad day in the Camp, when this was done, but there were no scenes and no disorder. Padre Negrini said a mass for the dead and camp life went on.

Meanwhile Albert's family had heard nothing of his whereabouts. With news of the sinking of the *Arandora Star* and the circumstances, Enrica remembers the strange calm that fell on Jessie and herself. "We knew that Albert would never have been among the fighters, and if he were on that ship, he must now have no more anguish to endure." [122] But soon after relief came. Jessie received a note written on the day Albert was arrested, and then another from which they learned that he was in a camp near Manchester, and still another saying he had been transferred to the Isle of Man.

Each day a small steamer delivered mail and newspapers from Liverpool. Albert constantly and eagerly scanned all the papers for news about the prospects of release. The *Manchester Guardian* and the *News Chronicle* were favourites, for they had taken up the cause.[123] Albert recounted that the name of Eleanor Rathbone, a British Member of Parliament who campaigned for their release, became sacred for many an internee who had lost faith in justice.[124]

"In fact, as Montano and I discussed again and again our position, we felt that all was not lost when it was still possible for anyone to take up the cause of 'enemy aliens' in the way in which these papers did."

And, so it proved. In late June they were told that petitions for release would now be received. Albert prepared his, in double copy, and handed it to the Camp Leader, who passed a copy to the Military Authorities. Captain Meyers, the Intelligence Officer, spoke encouragingly about his prospects of release, adding, however, that it would take time.

A few releases began to be authorized. But no response to Albert's application. Then a White Paper was published which stated that internees might be released on grounds of health, with those over 60 to be examined first. "When Montano urged me to apply for a medical examination I laughed. It is true that I had had sprue, dysentery and typhoid in China, but I had recovered and camp life did not seem harder for me than for others."

"Qui, bisogna provarle tutte,"[125] said Montano to me – "I urge you, I beg of you, to apply." Albert eventually applied and was examined, and, much to Albert's surprise, was told by the doctor that he would recommend his case to the Camp Medical Officer, Dr Jowett, as a suitable one for release on the grounds of health. On a never-to-be-forgotten morning, a few days later, a medical certificate, marked 'Urgent', was signed and forwarded to London.

"I moved about as if on wings, expecting to be released in two or three days. It was, however, nearly three weeks before the order arrived. It was dated August 15th, but did not reach the Camp till the 22nd."

It is impossible to describe the feeling that news of release brings to a captive, Albert wrote. "It has a magical effect. A few minutes after I heard the news, the whole internment episode began to look like a nightmare when one wakes."

The day was spent in handing over the business of the Welfare Committee, and the formalities connected with release. "There were about fifteen or sixteen of us, nearly all aged sixty or over. As we sat in the office, waiting to fill in the various forms, I was glad that no press-photographer was there, for a picture of our crowd might well have been used as anti-government propaganda."

He recalled Montano's comment when the first batch of old men had been set free. He had said: "Look at them! As a man, and from a humanitarian point of view, I am glad to see these fellows going home, but as an Italian at war with England, I am sorry, because it shows a return to common sense on the part of these people. You know, Padre, those old fellows here behind barbed-wire are a priceless advertisement for Germany and Italy. They are the evidence of what England really means when she talks about justice and fair play."

That night Albert could hardly sleep. Montano must have felt sad but he did not show it. "He asked me to send a message to his wife as soon as I could, urging her to leave the London district, and telling her that he was well."

"I count it as a privilege to have met Montano. Seldom have I come in contact with a better-informed man who could talk Italian, French and English with equal fluency and ease. His last hope for the world was Great Britain, but sometimes this hope was not very strong."

He could not forget or forgive the unpreparedness of Great Britain. "They knew it must come," he said, "and yet they would not tell the people of the danger."

He kept repeating Baldwin's famous excuse: "We would have lost the election." "That's it," he would say, pacing up and down the little room in the darkness, "We would have lost the election. To win the election was more important than to tell the truth about the deadly peril drawing nearer each day. Churchill was a voice crying in the wilderness, and yet there must have been those who knew he was right. You know, Garnier, if England goes down, there is nothing left for people like you and me."

Early next morning we gathered by the barbed-wire gates to say goodbye to our friends and to wait for the order to go to the wharf. People pressed around us on all sides. Albert was given a small leather bag, and a packet of butterscotch.

Someone wept, and another put both hands on his shoulders and just said: "E Allora!" There was something akin to agony in his eyes. He turned suddenly and went away. "As I said goodbye to another, I kissed him, Italian fashion, and he said with shining eyes: "I shall never forget the things we have talked about together." Padre Negrini was almost the last to speak to Albert. "God bless you, friend," he said.

"At the wharf there was a crowd of Germans, released like ourselves. Once on board we were free! I could not resist the temptation to pay the difference on our ticket and travel first class as far as Liverpool."

The crossing was rough, especially as they neared Liverpool, but Albert was not sick in spite of a substantial breakfast on board.

At Liverpool he caught a train which took him to Euston before 8pm. "During the whole of that journey a strange feeling of unreality was upon me. It was curious to be addressed by the only other occupant of my compartment, a Scottish lady, as an ordinary traveller. I wondered whether it was right for me not to say to her "Be Careful! I have only just been released from internment as an enemy alien."

"At Euston I phoned home to find that Enrica was there, but that Jessie had gone to a Thursday meeting at the Church. I arrived home close to 9pm, had a bath and went to bed."

It was August 23, 1940. "That first night of my return home is the only one I spent upstairs in bed, for the blitz intensified, and we have been sleeping on the floor in the dining room ever since."

Albert finished his fascinating account of war-time internment in February 1941 and he seems to have hardly ever mentioned it again. Certainly, he never raised internment in the many letters he wrote to me between 1952 and 1970. But, then again, his letters were from a grand-father to a grand-son who had 'lost' a father, and perhaps motivated by his own 'sense' of guilt (if that's the right word) of having sent Ben to boarding school at age eight and his own fatherless childhood, he understood my sense of loss. The account of his internment shows his modesty, humility and reluctance to push himself forward to take on the leadership roles he undertook successfully while interned. Given the opportunity, Albert was a man of action and which he communicated strongly in his letters. He cared.

… to dispiriting job as mail censor

After release from Isle of Man, Albert quickly resumed his role as pastor of the Coney Hill Baptist Church, in Kent – a happy experience, but short-lived. He took up full-time work as a censor for the British Post Office in Liverpool until the end of the war – a less than happy time.

While working at the highly confidential post of censor, he retained a moody silence and appeared low in spirits.[126] He later disclosed he had seen letters from Italy telling of the allied bombing on Turin and Milan, where his brother and extended family lived, and how people streamed out at night to sleep in barns and farmyards.

As a result of the air raids on Turin, the population of Torre Pellice increased from 5,000 to 7,000 during the war. They included many Waldensians who normally lived in Turin but returned during holidays, and others who rented houses usually left empty in the winter months, or found refuge in primitive huts and outhouses. Albert's mother's Malan family and his brother Emile, were among them for a time.

While working at the censor's office, Albert became aware of the intensive struggle that began in the mountain valleys reminiscent of the persecution that the Waldensians had endured in the Middle Ages, and where he was raised and loved to tramp.

During the 1930s and into the war years, the anti-Fascist movement had grown. While Albert was not directly involved, resistance to Mussolini's Italy had developed within the Waldensian community with the credo that "to think like a Fascist, was an immoral act." In Torre Pellice's Caffe Italia, located under the arcade, anti-Fascist talks were given to locals, and the town gradually became the headquarters of the resistance; a place in which politics, faith and armed conflict joined forces.

As news of the Armistice in 1943 [127] spread through the mountain villages, and signs that Germany wanted to entrench itself in Italy, the locals sensed a bloody conflict was in the making. They took from the abandoned Italian garrison weapons, ammunition and even horses to hide on their farms nearby. And the focus shifted to setting up partisan groups to resist the Germans as well as the Fascists.

On the afternoon the armistice was confirmed, the Waldensian Synod happened to be sitting in Torre Pellice. A member of a youth Christian movement, Gioventu Cristiana ("Christian Youth") – of which Albert's cousin Frida Malan was secretary – proposed that the Church formally condemn the Nazis and the Fascists. The synod conferred and refused. A distinct split was forming. As one of the younger members remarked: 'Our Vaudois Church today doubts, is wary, fears, trembles and buckles and adapts itself, and hides'. The individual pastors took note.[128]

Although there is no record of where Albert stood, his liberal-minded and freedom-loving views indicate he would have been dispirited by the abandonment of Waldensian moral certainty. Albert's Church seemed to have compromised its independence, 'freedom' values and faith in justice, but his principles sided with the actions of the local partisan groups. The partisans, including Emile and Malan family members, had quickly formed and established themselves in the Val Pellice mountains, including the caves in nearby Angrogna, close to the Malan and Garnier residences.

Years later, Vanna Garnier, wife of Ben and a member of the Malan family, took me and my wife Juliet to a spot in Torre Pellice where as a child she and others were forced to watch a Nazi execution of a partisan. Vanna's family had moved to Torre from Turin to escape the bombing; the family soon moved back to Turin till the war's end. I was also shown by relatives a photo of corpses of partisans hanging from lamp posts on the road to Villar Pellice (between Torre and Bobbio).[129] Most are buried in the cemetery at Torre Pellice, with photographs showing they were very young.

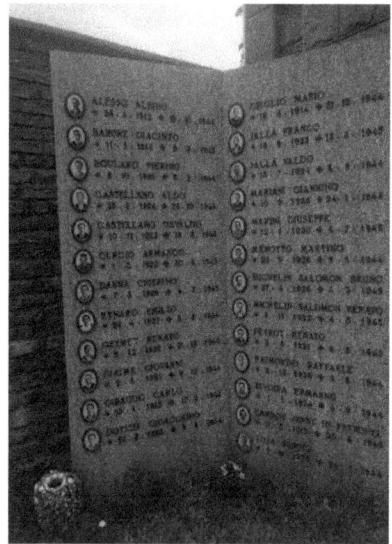

The headstone in Torre Pellice cemetery of 25 Waldensian partisans killed by "NaziFasciste" during World War II.

For Albert and other Waldensians, going back centuries, freedom and liberty were precious. He said often in China, in the Isle of Man and, I am sure, in Torre Pellice: "I don't have political ideas, only moral certainties."

On release from the Isle of Man retention, Albert judged it wise to take up British nationality, a five-year process, completed in 1948 – nearly nine years after son Ben's taking up British citizenship in 1939 prior to sailing to New Zealand.

As the war years disappeared, it would be the exploits of Ben in New Zealand, Africa and North America that would occupy Albert's mind, together with frequent visits to Torre Pellice.

Albert in summer discussion with brother Emile – Torre Pellice, 1950s. *"I don't have political ideas, only moral certainties."*

In 1948, Albert joined the British Broadcasting Corporation (BBC) as supervisor of the Chinese Section of the Far Eastern Department, a position he held for 14 years until age 80. From 1949 he was pastor to the Huguenot Congregation meeting for worship in French in the Crypt of Canterbury Cathedral. His last sermon was preached in November 1972. He was specially remembered at a service held in the Crypt on May 20th 1973.

PART THREE: **LOOKING BACK TO LOOK FORWARD**

Chapter 10:   BEN'S SOLUTION TO THREATS TO EARTH

DESPITE Ben's problematic personal life, he had a successful career and was among the earliest scientists to point to the evidence setting out the accelerating man-made climate change.

Ben's later research focused on other problems associated with the state of planet Earth. It was the bigger picture, and not just climate change that threatened mankind, he believed.

It seemed to Ben that ultimately the solution to Earth's problems depends on the workings of the human brain.

From an early age, he questioned his father putting "God" on a pedestal. Ben rejected his parents' religious beliefs, and was unhappy at Eltham boarding school. His brother Wallie spent time and energy consoling him.[130] Ben considered his father's claim that mankind is possessed of rights and duties which are derived from God and not from man was nonsense, and, in later life rejected the idea as unscientific.

While Albert accepted the truths of 'science' based on reason, his acceptance of rights and duties derived from God are based on faith – not reason. For Ben, duties derived from God haven't been, can't be, verified!

Ben put it this way: "If I write a paper and it goes to China, England, America or New Zealand, everybody in these places who reads it believes that I am telling the truth as I see it. Nobody assumes that what I am writing is true. But everybody knows that I write the scientific paper on an implicit, unwritten understanding among scientists that it can be absolutely believed to be what I believe." A theory of belief becomes knowledge (i.e., true) only after verification by testing.

Unfortunately, Ben noted, in today's world, that kind of easy endorsement does not apply in any other subject than science (and medicine) – not politics, religion or things about which people go to war. Science is no longer science if forced without evidence to achieve a particular end or conclusion.

Concerned, like Albert, at the possibility of nuclear war, Ben quoted scientist Albert Einstein that he had been taught that modern times began with the fall of the Roman Empire, but in fact they began with the fall of the bomb that destroyed Hiroshima.[131] While intra-nation warfare had previously caused 'limited' damage, it now puts the whole planet in jeopardy. Earth is the ultimate victim. Scientists had created the 'bomb', politicians had decided, and will decide, on its use.

The outcome of World War II reinforced Ben's view that large scale (nuclear) war was a losing proposition, and no longer appropriate in a world in which security must be mutual if mankind's survival was the aim.

Throughout his career as a scientist, Ben tried to educate non-scientists about how to evaluate the risks associated with various courses of action, since, technically, there is never certainty in science. It matters little whether the probability of a nuclear war causing nuclear winter is 5% or 95%; the consequences of the risk are the same. But decision-makers do not seem able to grasp this basic principle.

"Occasionally I imagine myself a newspaper reporter at a press conference with (say) the president of USA asking my question: Has the President considered proposing to the President of Russia that each party limit their nuclear capability to what is needed to blow up the world once, and if the President considers that more than this is needed for peace how does he propose the world should be blown up a second time? But for most of the time I just stay quiet (like I imagine most people do) because whatever one does everyone will die one day anyway!" Ben noted that many of mankind's greatest concepts came from ideas or hunches based on little information. In science, where hunches must have formal rigour, we find theories about the physical world which are on trial awaiting more evidence to strengthen, modify, or subvert them. Many 'facts' are the creation of ideas; but those who grant a high intellectual priority to information assume that facts, all by themselves, can overtake and unseat ideas.

As a teacher, Ben knew that a question cannot be answered until it has been asked; and, a question cannot be asked until there is someone to 'think' to ask it.

He came to believe that assumptions on how the universe works, its physical laws, are because of the way the human mind, more particularly the neocortex, works.[132]

He noted the discovery that the human brain has evolved through three stages (See diagram):

◊ Reptilian – selecting homesites, establishing territory, engaging in display, hunting, homing, mating, selecting leaders;

◊ Limbic system – following proven pathways, operating to a schedule, obedience to precedence, ceremony, religious convictions, legal actions, political persuasions, returning home to die;

◊ Neocortex – the brain of reading, writing and arithmetic: solving technical issues, asking questions.

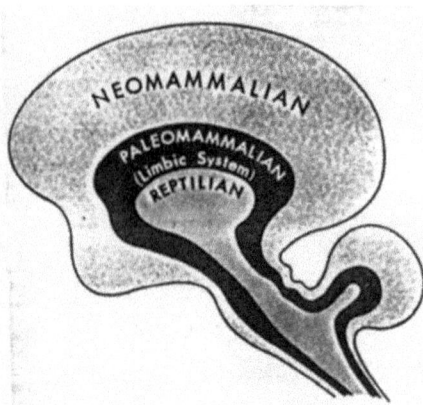

While the *old brain* (the 'reptilian' and 'limbic system' brains together) has been hardly touched by evolution, the neomammalian (*neocortex*) of humans expanded in the last half a million years at an explosive speed which is without precedent in the history of evolution.

The findings of science through the logic of the fossil record, shows that humans, with our intelligence, our technology and our power, are not the stewards of planet Earth. In fact, we are the most recently-arrived tenants. Humans (homo sapiens) evolved about 200,000 years ago, barely a second on the evolutionary time-scale. We are at the start of a journey. If we are to survive and enjoy the journey we must learn to move past our unruly and destructive ways, and look to the future, not look back to the past. Ben spent time assessing how this might be achieved, believing the 'answer' lay in better use of our brains.

Decisions on the use of scientific knowledge are essentially a matter for politics and innovative businesses. This emphasizes the urgency for an effort by all nations, to work together for world-wide enlightenment of self-knowledge, to replace the 'enlightenment' of our western bulldozer culture.

The vital question in politics (and big business) is not 'WHO should rule?' but "HOW can we minimize misrule – both the likelihood of its occurring and, when it does occur, its consequences".

Late in his life, Ben asked me if I had read any Koestler. I had, *Janus: A Summing up.*[133] Ben quoted from Arthur Koestler – "one of the central features of the human predicament is the overwhelming capacity and need for identification with a social group and/or system of beliefs, which is indifferent to reason, indifferent to self-interest, and even to the claim of self-preservation."

The crucial point is, said Koestler, that in creating the human brain, evolution has wildly overshot the mark.[134]

In the popular language of today, our three brains might be thought of as biological computers, each with its own peculiar form of subjectivity and its own intelligence, its own sense of time and space and its own memory, motor and other functions. [135]

The 'reptilian' and 'limbic system' brains together, for the sake of simplicity, we may call the 'old brain', as opposed to the neocortex, the specifically human 'thinking cap'. While the *old brain* has been hardly touched by evolution, the *neocortex* of humans (hominoids) expanded in the last half a million years at an explosive speed which is without precedent in the history of evolution. The new-brain explosion seems to have followed the type of exponential curve which has recently become familiar to us – population explosion, information explosion, technology explosion etc.

"Thus, the brain explosion gave rise to a mentally unbalanced species in which old brain and new brain, emotion and intellect, faith and reason, were at loggerheads. On one side, the pale cast of rational thought, of logic suspended on a thin thread all too easily broken; on the other, the raging fury of passionately held irrational beliefs, reflected in the holocausts of past and present history." [136]

With respect to Koestler, Ben and I agreed on some notable symptoms of the mental disorder which threaten continued human existence:

◊ The persistent pursuit of intra-nation warfare which, while earlier on could cause limited damage, now thanks to nuclear technology puts the whole planet in jeopardy;

◊ The split between rational and irrational thinking, affecting basic beliefs threatening mankind's longevity – (the nuclear threat and inability to manage; and, I am sure, Covid-19 protests; Russia's invasion of Ukraine);

◊ The contrast between mankind's genius in conquering Nature and its ineptitude in (sustainably) managing its own affairs – e.g. the space race, deforestation and, especially, CO_2 generation driving climate change;

◊ The population explosion, now threatening extinction of numerous species – leading to the 6th Extinction, in which Earth continues on without a human population.

"In a single century the population doubles; then it doubles again, and then again. Vast forests are razed. Humans do this deliberately, in order to feed themselves. Less deliberately; they shift organisms from one continent to another, reassembling the biosphere. No creature has ever altered life on the planet in this way before. In pushing other species to extinction, humanity is busy sawing off the limb on which it perches." [137]

These phenomena are specifically and uniquely human, and not found in other species. It therefore seems logical that our search for responses should also focus on those attributes of *homo sapiens* which are exclusively human and not shared by the rest of the animal kingdom.

Why has learning to use our 'new' brains been so slow? Koestler suggested the 'old' brain got in the way of, or acted as a brake on, the new.[138] Europe's retreat into the so-called Dark Ages, the 100-years war, and China's Manchu feudalism are historic examples.

Ben mentioned the work in China of Joseph Needham, a fellow Cambridge graduate, who wrote a series of books first published in 1954 titled *Science and Civilization in China*. Needham spent many years in China from about 1943 asking questions, and discovered some 600-plus inventions spanning 5,000 years (including printing, gunpowder, the compass, blast furnaces, suspension bridges, chess). "The mere fact of seeing them listed brings home to one the astonishing inventiveness of the Chinese people," said Needham.

More than that, the encyclopedia, or *Yongle Dadian*, completed in 1421 comprising all Chinese knowledge from the previous 2,000 years includes sections on geography, cartography, agriculture, civil and military engineering, warfare, health, medical care, plus other subjects, and, of particular interest to Ben, mathematics and astronomy.

Needham describes the depth of Chinese mathematical knowledge from the year A.D. 263 onward.[139] There are mathematical methods for calculating the area and volume of circles, spheres, cones, pyramids, cubes and cylinders. There is practical advice on using trigonometry to determine the height of buildings, trees, hills and the circumference of walled cities, the depth of ravines, and the breadth of river estuaries.

A *Shoushi* calendar produced by Chinese astronomer Guo Shoujing was officially adopted by the Ming Bureau of Astronomy in 1384. To predict the length of the year at 365.2425 days, which is accurate to within 10 seconds a year, Guo Shoujing must have known how the solar system worked, including the facts that the earth travels around the sun in an ellipse and is not at the centre of the universe and that the earth is attracted to the sun's much bigger mass. His calculations for the lunar month of 29.530593 days required complex trigonometry.

The *Shoushi* calendar contained a mass of astronomical data running to thousands of observations. It enabled comets and eclipses to be predicted for years ahead, as well as times of sunrise and sunset, moonrise and moonset.[140]

As Needham points out, the Chinese voyages of the 1400s to Italy were based on the idea of sharing the advanced knowledge and inventions the Chinese had acquired, and yet it was Europe (and later America) that took them up and developed the industrial and technological revolutions, while China went backward, retreating into a feudal (and later a communist) system. Why?

Needham never fully worked out the answers. However, Ben noted that China specialist, E. T. C. Werner suggested in 1922 that the "zeal" for orthodox learning, combined with the literary test for office in the Emperor's Court, "was the reason why scientific knowledge was prevented from developing." [141] Entrepreneurship and creative thinking were stifled by a compliant bureaucracy. It was a failure to use the brain to its full capacity. The 'old' brain got in the way of, or acted as a brake on, the new?

Ben suggests this is something for science and education to explore, noting that all previous generations of mankind have had to come to terms with the prospect of his/her death as an individual; the present generation is the first to face the prospect of the death of our species.

Koestler: The scientific community has pitifully failed to define this predicament of man. The evolution of the human brain is the only example of evolution providing a species with an organ which it does not know how to use. "We treat our brain as a luxury organ, which will take its owner thousands of years to learn to put to proper use – if we ever do." [142] Really? Ben's response was: Why not learn how to use our brain properly?

Looming over the world is a great unanswered question: *What is science really for?* In 1965, Needham argued that we are living through a terrible period of misuse of applied science.[143] "Perhaps several centuries hence," he suggested, "the chief meaning of democracy will be seen to lie in the question whether or not science is used primarily *for people.*"

'Science for science's sake' seems only too often to cloak the conceptions of 'Science for the sake of big profits', and 'Science for the sake of defense' (i.e., the piling up of armaments). Needham agreed that science will never flourish in a stifling atmosphere of government control, "but under private corporate enterprise its utilization primarily for the benefit of people as a whole seems often far from obvious."

Ben and Needham were part of the lucky post-war Golden Age generation of 'free thinking' knowledge hunters who crisscrossed the world in search of scientific truths about the Earth, how it works and its health.

Through his volumes of *Science and Civilization in China,* Needham showed post-war Europeans, Americans and the Chinese themselves, that during the first 14 centuries of the Christian era, China offered a host of inventions and discoveries, which Europeans had little knowledge of where they originated.

For Ben, science was the dictate of what is true, false or unproven. Through research he worked out that the brain of people dictates the life they lead, leading to a belief that if intelligence is our only edge, therefore we must learn to use it better, to sharpen it, to understand its limitations and deficiencies.

Science confirms that humans hold 99.9% of our DNA sequences in common. We are far more closely related to one another than we are to any other animal. The Olympic Games, which China has successfully hosted, reinforce that we all are cut from the same cloth, made on the same pattern, granted the same strengths and weaknesses, and will ultimately share the same fate. Given the reality of our mutual interdependence, our intelligence, and what is at stake, are we really unable to break out of behaviour patterns evolved to benefit our ancestors of long ago? Or, more positively, are we ready to stake out a sustainable future for mankind as a whole?

Ben's treatise ended with reference to Carl Popper's *The Open Society and its Enemies*: There is no freedom if it is not secured by the State; and, conversely only a State controlled by free citizens can offer any reasonable security at all.

Popper, who lived and wrote *The Open Society* in New Zealand in the early 1940s, when Ben had recently arrived and was in his 20s, argued that the best society we can have, from a practical as well as moral point of view, is one which extends the maximum possible freedom to its members.[144]

The maximum freedom, however, is a qualified one – it can be created and sustained at optimum level only by institutions designed for that purpose and backed by the power of the state. This involves large-scale state intervention in political, economic and social life. But it is a philosophy of social democracy, for above all else it is about how to change things, and to do so in a way which, unlike violent revolution, is rational and humane.[145] The guiding principle for public policy put forward in *The Open Society* is the opposite: 'Minimise avoidable suffering'.

For Ben this was insufficient. The commitment to minimize avoidable suffering is very much a work in progress. Success will require an evolutionary leap to make greater use of 'new brain' thinking and seek actions designed to minimize the impact of issues where the continued existence of humanity and other species is on the line.

In the dawn of brain research, we have in the new brain (neo cortex) a mechanism to deal with the difficult medical and social problems of our time. The most challenging issue, however, is the problem of controlling our reptilian brain's intolerance, struggle for territory and unabated extinction of species, while at the same time finding a means of regulating our soaring population, modifying global deforestation and man-made CO_2 generation driving climate change.

We are 'almost' the most responsible generation in history in terms of our attempts to limit the possibility of global warfare, but percentages matter little. We want to avoid territorial and national conflict, which seems to be based on the natural predisposition of human beings to form hostile groups and expand at the expense of real or imagined enemies. But it is taking too long, the cost and energy required to achieve this is enormous. The United Nations for instance are an extremely complicated and tremendously expensive diplomatic network. The global climate change initiative is slow going and costly. Peaceful coexistence does not (yet) come 'naturally'.

What are the grounds for hope? If combined with the accumulated self-knowledge, our neocortical intelligence will continue to evolve, and cope with the mounting crises of our time. We have been able to continue to survive only because of the continuing evolution of our brains more than anything else.

Ben concluded our conversation that if he had his time again, instead of geography – and advocating successfully to the NZ Education Department in 1946 and elsewhere that geography be taught across the secondary school curriculum; and teaching the subject at university – he would recommend that learning how the brain works – biological order, mental creativity and our behaviour – become a core subject at secondary school. [146]

What would the students learn? Not just about the structure of the brain, but its ability to unify different cultural traditions to be able to live and prosper together peacefully. All three brains must intermesh and function together. The human brain with its creative capability, even though it is divided between a holistic mode of perception and linear numeracy, has evolved as an instrument of survival. Humans are now an endangered species, because of threats of our own making, because, crudely, we haven't used our brains properly.

But the global rise in the awareness of threat, and the race underway to create new societies with high survival values is itself a new exponential. The old order is dying but it is slow going. Territorial conflicts continue. If the world has thrown religious sanctions out of the window, can we afford to kick even ethics downstairs? Perhaps the whole world as well as China, as it attempts to rise to world dominance for a second time, needs Confucius, Buddhism, Taoism, Islam, and Protestantism more desperately than ever.

Ben and Albert would probably agree. And what about China's and the world's leadership?

Chapter 11:   ALBERT ON SAVING CHINA'S 'SOUL'

ALBERT left China in the late-1930s "thrilled" at having witnessed the re-birth of a mighty nation, but 90 years later the shape of China's spiritual dimension to take the country and world forward – body, mind and spirit – is still uncertain.

As Japan invaded China and World War II commenced, Albert along with many Chinese knew little of China's early world-leading scientific-led know-how era and its principled transfer to Italy in the 1400s.

Likewise, Albert and Chinese and the rest of mankind, were ignorant of the scale of scientific 'progress' emerging and which by the 2020s, threatened continued human existence on Earth. The role that our three-part brain plays in dictating violent versus peaceful behaviour and environmentally threatening versus sustainable decision making was unknown.

But today's China is different. With the higher living standards across the country, it is once again becoming scientifically-led, education-focused, creative, and inventive – qualities that Albert would support. China's 14th Five-Year Plan (2021-2025) and long-range objectives through 2035 kicks off a new journey to build a modern socialist country.

There is clear evidence of application of strategic 'new brain' thinking aimed at achieving some sustainable, peaceful long-term goals: From the Silk Road to the Space Race, from Antarctica to traditional Chinese medicine, President Xi Jinping is chasing his/China's dream of a great renewal of the Chinese world [147] – *Zhong Go Meng*. The Plan includes systematic protection and publication of key ancient books,[148] construction of a Renaissance Library and world-class tourist destinations across China.

Xi Jinping's "socialism with Chinese characteristics" incorporates a game plan to "establish China as a rich, strong, democratic, civilised, harmonious, beautiful modernized social world power." The 'soul' of China is no-longer, if it ever was, (just) a matter of religion, but an ideology and culture tied with the 14th Five-Year Plan's 2035 objective to achieve 'common prosperity for all'.[149] The long-term objective is to control and lift the workers' standard of living (as it has been in other 'caring' societies too).

But it will take patience, and won't be easy to capture the hearts and minds of the world's public, let alone successive generations in China.

As Albert found between 1911 and the 1930s, and I experienced on visits, including to Taiwan, in the 1980s, and others have recently reconfirmed, Chinese become, understandably, upset when reminded of the indignities suffered by 'foreign devils' between the Opium Wars and establishment of Communist

China in 1949. Also, China is almost alone in the world. Relationships with neighbours are insecure (including Russia?), decades-long territorial disputes are unresolved, and collaboration with other world leaders appears difficult.

But because the Chinese leadership seems to have a passionate desire to see China justified in the eyes of the world, it may be ready to play a role that is more cautious, conciliatory, and co-operative than it has in the recent past?

Naïve! Perhaps, but the 14th Five-Year plan published in 2021 headlines promotion of 'the peaceful development' of cross-strait relations and Taiwan's reunification of the motherland. "We will adhere to the One-China Principle and take the *well-being* of compatriots on both sides of the Taiwan Strait as the *goal*."

If the words are to be taken seriously, then protecting and possibly enhancing the 'well-being' of all Chinese (and therefore the rest of the world's population) is the primary 'goal'.

True, China has strong military capabilities, but its primary concern in its published Plan and Strategy is defence. It will continue to resist invading Taiwan (or other countries or challenging the military supremacy of the United States.)[150] Or will it?

For many Chinese themselves reunification with Taiwan is a primary 'spiritual' goal.

China has been only partially independent since 1949. It still has to get Taiwan back into the 'central kingdom' and won't be spiritually 'together' until that 'rebirth' happens. Xianggang (Hong Kong) and Aomen (Macao) are almost reunited politically and spiritually. But whether Taiwan's reunification will happen through peaceful means remains unclear.

During my visit to mainland China, I was surprised how often the reunification topic was raised. I was frequently asked what I thought! By the trip's end, my response went roughly as follows: Reunification is inevitable. I told how I had detected on a Taiwan visit some years previously, a yearning by the post-war generation of Han Chinese to "one day before I die" visit the ancestral homelands in China's mainland provinces.

Perhaps Taiwan's leadership could be encouraged to initiate a face-saving 'peaceful' formula reunification negotiation, along the lines of 'one country, two systems', with some autonomy as other regions of China enjoy? Again, perhaps naïve, especially given the apparent pushiness of the United States to keep Taiwan close.

If Taiwan declared independence, however, then China would probably invade. But in many Chinese eyes this would not be perceived as aggressive – it would be done to defend sacred historic borders. Meanwhile the bottom line is that the concept for the peaceful reunification of China's mainland and Taiwan still applies.[151]

Yes, what happens to Taiwan over the next few years will have wide implications for China's future, the ultimate legacy of Albert's 30 years in China and our future too, I suspect!

The overwhelming weight of China's population may perpetuate the ambition for China to play a dominating role in world affairs. For a country with a third of the world's population that would be difficult to challenge.

"Time and momentum are on our side," Xi told Committee officials on 11 January 2021. "Our circle of friends is constantly growing; the balance of history is tilting toward China."

A "Brief History of the Communist Party" praises Xi for bringing China "closer to the centre of the world stage than it has ever been. The nation has never been closer to its own rebirth." [152]

The reference to China's 'rebirth' is telling. The aim is to create a modern socialist democracy with ordinary Chinese enjoying advanced living standards. But more than that, by force of numbers and strength of culture, China could become, once again, a new moral source and spiritual civilisation in the world, perhaps forming a dominate wedge between Russia and United States (and European Union?).

Is China's 'rebirth' a progressive and unifying step, or a backward leap in terms of bringing China to the centre of the world stage?

Xi seems to want to create a new world order. He is on target with the economy, with science, with education. His attitude, or, more accurately, his success in re-defining and unifying the 'soul' of China will perhaps be his biggest test.

Certainly, Xi's transformational leadership of China to rebuild the 'soul' of China and create an innovative, prosperous nation will be tested by events outside as well as inside China. In mid-June 2021 the G7 (including US President Biden) agreed to confront "systemic challenges to the rules-based world order" as they saw them emanating from China. They agreed to respond to China together, including to its "New Silk Road Initiative", its territorial conflicts in the South and East China Seas, its actions in Hong Kong and toward Taiwan, and its domestic human rights violations.

How China behaves between now and 2049 – and perhaps longer – has a lot to do with the West (United States, Europe and Russia). Many of the tensions in modern-day China are eternal, but so is the country's resourcefulness.

A big question is whether the ultimate future of China is to be based on a continued (anti-western, anti 'foreign devils') inward-looking perspective, or a return to a progress of history 'giving of knowledge' (circa 1400s) to the world – an evolution garnered from 'new-brain' thinking and leadership?

Internally, Xi's 'common prosperity for all' and 'reunification' agenda coupled with the recent extension of his authoritarian leadership term indefinitely, has been likened to a revival of a traditional Chinese empire intending to remain in power "pretty much for ever". [153]

Plainly, nothing is settled. It never is. That is the nature of evolution and China conforms to that pattern of life.

In the ultra-modernised China of today, a religious resurgence is underway. It is happening, slowly, after a rocky, bumpy start, and the ultimate outcome is far from certain. I am no professional China watcher, but I detect that China's leadership is looking back into its rich history for the spiritual guidance to, step-by-step, take China and the world forward – body, mind and spirit. [154]

In 1945, Albert wrote of some 'encouraging signs' that China might eventually find inspiration in Christianity for the future, but he set out one condition:

"The Christianity which will make its greatest appeal to the Chinese people is the Christianity that will be understood as 'good news' for all, and for the whole of every person – body, mind and spirit.

"Its standard of conduct must not be inferior to that demanded of the best follower of Confucius; its spirit of worship must surpass that of the most devout Buddhist; while its devotion to an ideal must not fall short of that of the most ardent follower of Karl Marx.

"An easy-going Christianity, indifferent to the material welfare of mankind, or afraid of the discoveries of modern science, or divided against itself, or even devoted exclusively to the salvation of the soul after death, without apparent concern for the practice of righteousness in this world, will not be the religion to which the Chinese will turn for the building up of the nation." [155]

However, Albert was keenly aware that a large number of Chinese simply do not care one way or the other for Christian worship – they are completely indifferent to it. "They may be impressed by some Christian institutions, such as schools and hospitals, but they are quite disinterested in it as a power bearing on everyday life."

The younger generation especially, are either critical or antagonistic: "A knowledge of science and of the writings of some of our Western scientists and philosophers leads them to discard everything that cannot be proved by the light of reason."

Like the majority of Western youth, including his youngest son Ben, Chinese youth were religious sceptics – atheists.

Albert recounts that he had often been questioned by students, "How can you ask me, a young man of the China of to-day, to believe in God? Have you read any science? Is your thinking up-to-date? And as for a God of justice and love, how can you believe that He exists when the world is what it is? What about injustice among men? What of floods, famines, earthquakes? And what about war? Even if you could prove to me that a God does exist, what difference would it make when all these things are happening in our times? You speak of the power of Christ to heal diseases and to help men; well, what has happened to that power?"

And Albert concedes that many Chinese were turning to Christianity because of what missionaries practiced (rather than what they preached), noting that during the years of unrest following the 1911 Revolution there was a common saying that the country suffered from three kinds of 'plagues' – floods, droughts and warlords. "Individual Christians, missionaries and churches were always among the first to help in these calamities, and the people began to turn to Christianity in consequence."

When the Republic was established in 1949 under Chairman Mao Zedong, China was declared an atheist state. In the "New China" that Albert correctly foresaw coming, neither the Chinese past was embraced or Western civilization adopted.

However, both Protestantism and Catholicism (rather than Christianity, which includes the Orthodox religions) were added to the list of long-standing Chinese 'religions' of Taoism, Buddhism and Islam. The religious radio station established when Albert was head of the Society, the expanded Bible printing and distribution programmes and the community help work probably influenced the decision to establish Protestantism as an acceptable stand-alone religion, as later numbers reinforced.

After the Mao era repression, Deng Xiaoping opened up religious practice, moving China away from strict anti-religious Marxism. Meanwhile Xi Jinping has launched a third new and more nuanced but still evolving era in the history of the communist party's religious policy.

In recent years, many religious traditions have re-established, and, despite periodic repression, churches, mosques and temples have been rebuilt and clergy trained.

A 2011 BBC report conservatively estimated that there were 60 million Christians in China (compared with 1 million in 1949). Small Protestant 'house churches' are especially having a strong impact on the country.

By 2021, Protestant Christianity was probably the fastest-growing faith, according to *The Economist*, although most religious Chinese practice the longer-standing foreign import of Buddhism and traditional Taoism.[156]

The huge number of Protestants, 38-50 million, up from around 22 million a decade earlier, compared with 10-12 million Catholics, has been linked to China's rising living standards.

The growth in religion has accompanied China's rapid economic expansion over the last 20 years. Now the world's second largest economy, China illustrates how even a limited amount of economic freedom has the power to lift millions of Chinese out of abject poverty and build one of the strongest economies in the world.

The booming Protestant numbers in China, have been associated with China's adoption of the protestant work ethic.[157] In a blog about Christianity and western civilisation, economic historian Niall Ferguson, defines the ethic as: *A moral (or spiritual) framework – a mode of activity derived primarily from the teaching of Protestant reformers.*

Ferguson argues that the protestant work ethic provides "a measure of stability and duty to balance the dynamic and potentially unstable values created by competition in a consumer society." He postulates that the ethic has been abandoned in its birthplace of Western Europe and also the United States, but is alive and well in China.

He suggests that China is starting to supplant the West, but is doing it by becoming more Western. This is only partly true. China's resurgence is also about capturing "New China's" spirit of nationalism by modifying Marxist socialism and adopting traditional "Chinese characteristics". Ancient Chinese values involve a spiritual dimension that is uniquely Chinese, but which reflects the protestant work ethic – a workforce that is more learned, willing to work longer hours and seeks to save more of their earnings than their counterparts in other parts of the world.

It harks back to ancient Chinese practice of the 13th and 14th centuries of work, wealth creation and spirit of the Silk Road; and, let's not forget, it reflects the best-practice (as distinct from preaching) of late 19th and early 20th century Protestant missionaries in China.

Protestant missionaries in China, like Albert, as we have seen, opened the first modern schools and universities, established the first hospitals and clinics, provided the first training for nurses, worked to abolish feudal-era practices such as foot binding and improve treatment of maids. They launched charitable work and distributed food to the poor. They also opposed the opium trade and brought treatment to many who were addicted, and helped with recovery during wartime with Japan. They worked hard to care for the body, mind and spirit of ordinary Chinese. They preached and practiced a Protestant ethic. They cared for the wellbeing of ordinary Chinese.

What they practiced was backed by evidence in the results, what they preached less so!

In *Souls of China: The Return of Religion After Mao*, Ian Johnson, a Pulitzer-Prize winning writer focusing on society, religion, and history,[158] in 2017 observed that: "Following a century of violent anti-religious campaigns, China is now filled with new temples, churches and mosques – as well as cults, sects and politicians trying to harness religion for their own ends. Driving this explosion of faith is uncertainty – over what it means to be Chinese, and how to live an ethical life in a country that discarded traditional morality a century ago and is still searching for new guideposts."

In *God is Back* looking at the spiritual revival in China, John Micklethwait and Adrian Wooldridge open with reference to a Bible study in Shanghai, where the Chinese pastor proclaims: *"In Europe the church is old. Here it is modern. Religion is a sign of higher ideals and progress. Spiritual wealth and material wealth go together. That is why we will win."* [159]

Does it mean Albert's "God is Back" – No and Maybe.

No – Most Chinese (like the majority of people worldwide) are atheists. And the current state of religious freedom in China is far from perfect or truly free. There are issues with many religions that fall outside the state-sanctioned sphere of influence.

As religious faiths have grown, the government has tightened its oversight in an effort to eliminate possible sources of political dissent or secession, and embarked on a carefully planned 'spiritual' alignment movement.

Government-approved versions of traditional Buddhism, Taoism, Protestant and Catholic faiths have been promoted, and those seen as politically threatening have been repressed.

Maybe – In the sense that religion is now a matter of choice for most people, and is not forced or inherited. Those attending a church in Shanghai may well believe in God, the saviour. However, the protestant work ethic is not a religious concept, but it is "a way of life" linking body, mind and spirit that many observers of China believe both Protestant's and Buddhist's align with in pursuit of a healthy, liveable Chinese economy.[160] Buddhism is a religion without a God; many of those who practice the Protestant ethic do so without any belief in a God.

While Albert was more concerned to save individual souls than 'convert China' to Protestantism (Christianity), it was nonetheless the wellbeing of China that Albert deeply cared for, which is clearly a concern of China's current leader Xi Jinping.

In writing about the emerging "New China" in 1945, Albert referred to a book by Dr San Yet Sen, *The San Min Chu I,* as a publication "which may almost be called the Bible of the Nationalist Party in China". The new spirit of China must be guided along three lines – "first, a return to ancient Chinese morality, based on loyalty, filial piety, clarity, faithfulness, justice and love of peace; secondly, a return to ancient Chinese wisdom, based on the teaching of *The Great Learning,* to the effect that in order to manage well the affairs of State, it is necessary to 'regulate the family', 'to cultivate one's person', to 'rectify one's heart', to be 'sincere in one's thinking', and to 'extend one's knowledge to the utmost'; and thirdly, on the cultivation of Western science."

Will Xi adopt this approach? Taoism has reportedly been allowed to flourish, and since taking office President Xi has met with Buddhist leaders.[161] China also recently released a major plan to improve social morality for the first time since 2001.

As of 2018, one of the goals for "promoting Chinese Christianity" is "thought reform". The plan calls for "retranslating and annotating" the Bible, to find commonalities with Chinese socialism and establish a "correct understanding" of the text.

Numerous versions of the Bible have been produced in China over the years, but how altering the Bible's text will help the sinicization of Christianity is far from clear.

Albert 'translated' a protestant version of the Bible into Chinese text, and would be appalled at the intrusion of China's government into the process. A core Waldensian tenet is the separation of Church and state.

The only Bible publisher in China (Amity Printing Company) in 2019 celebrated a milestone as the 200 millionth copy was printed. The Nanjing-based publisher opened a new factory in 2008 with capacity to print a million Bibles a month. The company exports, and has offices in Hong Kong and Geneva.

As Ian Johnson comments, Xi's social morality plan stems from a widespread feeling that China's relentless desire for economic development has created a mental vacuum, sometimes leading to blatant rule-breaking and trampling on civilization. There is a lack of trust between people.

China is entering a more uncertain era, with slower economic growth and rising inequality, while Beijing is giving itself a traditional cloak to broaden its appeal, suggests Johnson. He might have added that returning to pre-1911 thinking aligns with the aim of reunifying China, and which is clearly on Xi Jinping's 2035 agenda.

The government blueprint for dealing with this moral crisis, calls for recognition of certain traditional beliefs. While the Xi plan cites communist slogans such as "socialist core values", it calls China's history a "rich moral resource", in stark contrast to the last document in 2001 that only occasionally mentioned Chinese traditions. The new plan calls on party officials to promote the "ancient sages" and to expound "in-depth" traditional concepts such as "benevolence", "justice" and "righteousness and courage".

It makes no mention of Mao Zedong and his successors, or their ideology, but instead focuses on Xi Jinping and his efforts to tackle social problems such as gold worship and hedonism. This work is not intended to replace Communism with Confucianism or Protestantism. Instead, China will likely remain a secular (atheist) nation. It is fair to say, however, that this is the first time since the collapse of the feudal Dynasty in 1911 that the central government has accepted the idea that the political-religious order that formed China for much of the past 2,500 years has been re-accepted. Why? This is not only to address China's moral vacuum, *but also* a populist measure.

The next five years will likely see expansion of Chinese education and socialism. This will be a process to create a spiritual civilization through a "new era" based on Xi Jinping Thought on Socialism with Chinese Characteristics. [162]

Over the last 20 years, China has eradicated extreme poverty. It now, seemingly, wants to eliminate extreme wealth. While the future direction of introducing 'common prosperity for all' is not yet clear, Xi Jinping has declared that "we must not allow the gap between rich and poor to get wider" and warned that "it is unrealistic to expect a peaceful life without struggle."

The 14th Five-year Plan combines its policy to promote innovation-driven growth with the creation of a modern welfare state. A pilot scheme to deliver Common Prosperity in Zhejiang province (population 65 million, and home of Alibaba) includes more spending on social services – and substantial 'donations' from local billionaires.

Xi Jinping promises construction by 2035 of "a peaceful and secure China" with "common prosperity for all".[163] Does this promised 'prosperity' embrace both the material and spiritual well-being of all? And how does this agenda 'fit' with Albert's version of the kind of religion likely to have the greatest appeal in the 'New China', a term he used in 1945? [164]

As a teenager, Xi was sent to the countryside under Mao's regime; he lived in a cave in Shanxi province, working as a peasant farmer by day and studying the works of Mao by night, and while his parents in Beijing were allegedly in prison. What impact did this have on him, and the development of his beliefs and world view?

The Chinese know Xi Jinping is no fool. He has led China on a journey of reform – beaten extreme poverty, tackled corruption, sought a broad-based democratic responsiveness and participation in preparing the 14th Five-year Plan and 2035 action agenda. He is a strategist. He seems to be in touch with the issues facing the world. He seems to be a peace seeker and strongly supports improvements of the Chinese worker's lifestyle and living standards.

What Xi seems to be doing is stepping towards establishing a social democracy. 'Seems' is the operative word, because China is still very much a one-party state, as under Mao, a one-man show.

In 2017, Xi Jinping claimed that China stood "tall and firm in the east", and it was now time for China "to transform itself into a mighty force" that could lead the world on political, economic, military and environmental issues.[165]

When will China take action to transform itself, as Xi promised in 2017? This is something to watch for, possibly in the context of Russia's invasion of Ukraine and whether, and how, China pursues its Taiwan aspirations.

Meanwhile what would Albert and Ben make of Xi Jinping's sayings and actions? Ben would likely support China's focus on education and scientific outcomes, and possibly Albert the promise to return to using the Chinese classic philosophers. Albert would support Xi's promise to look at the Bible for inspiration, and help by pointing to the relevant passages. Both would be appalled at the treatment of the Uyghurs minority in western China. Both would support the actions to raise living standards and beat poverty, and want this to continue.

After returning to Europe from China in 1937, Albert said at the end of World War II that Western man's overwhelming control of natural processes in the atomic age had outstripped his own moral strength and psychological development. In Ben's terms, Western leaders arguably lack the insight to allow the 'new brain' to dominate the 'old brain'. The territorial imperative continues to drive decisions, as does the advances of science without constraint. And the East? Is China's leadership charting to 'lead the world' to a sustainable or destructive future – evolution or revolution?

It was primarily to save the soul of China that Albert spent 30 years in China, by which he meant that individual Chinese take their inspiration from the religion of Jesus Christ. [166]

That hasn't happened, despite China in the early 1950s adopting both

Protestantism and Catholicism as 'official' religions – along with Taoism, Buddhism and Islam.

Albert's idea that China's soul could be saved by adopting the religion of Jesus Christ was highly implausible. It is a version of the pursuit of Empire building based on a selective, codified 'foreign' faith. That unverified, unverifiable laws of a Christian God be adopted by the State ignores other major, traditional religious forces at work in China – Confucianism and Buddhism. The two Christian faiths – Protestantism and Catholicism – recognized by the Chinese State are accepted to the extent that they are no longer identified as part of the imperialism of the West.

Albert (1945): "They saw in us missionaries, people who had come to deceive them, so that China might fall an easy prey to the imperialism of Western countries. 'You come with the Gospel of Matthew in one hand, and a sword in the other,' was their cry." [167]

Albert's summary is accurate. But his belief system is arguably no longer appropriate in today's world; it has been superseded by growth of a single, interdependent global civilization created by the discoveries of science, but which is increasingly losing its way.

While the literal truth of Albert's belief system might be highly questionable, the underlying ethical and moral principles surely still hold. And it is these principles that China's leadership is (still) searching for, both for applying within China and globally.

Albert and Ben would also want China to hold true to its 'peaceful' approach in delivering its imperialistic objectives. If intelligence is our only edge, therefore they would both expect China's and the world's leadership to (quickly) learn to use it better, to sharpen it, to understand its limitations and deficiencies, and then to act.

Russia and the United States are continuing with 'them' and 'us' leadership. Meanwhile Xi's response to Putin's invasion of Ukraine is unclear – it leaves open options. How China eventually copes with Putin-Russia's Ukraine crusade could well be key. As the *New York Times*, of 16 March 2022, put it: Xi has avoided criticizing Putin, but he has also tried to distance China from the carnage. China has denounced the international sanctions imposed on Russia but hinted that Chinese companies may comply with them. This would protect China's economic interests in the West. Xi has warned the Kremlin against using nuclear weapons, and also apparently offered to assist in negotiating a settlement.

In the end, China's leadership has calculated that it must try to rise above what it considers a struggle between two tired powers and be seen as a pillar of stability in an increasingly turbulent world.

If Xi truly believes "the greatest dream of the Chinese people in modern history is the great renewal of the Chinese nation", [168] he must understand the global threats exposed by Russia's carnage and that we, mankind, are all in this together. Time and momentum are no longer on China's side, and the balance of history is no longer tilting towards China. Putin has made sure of that and he must be confronted. Xi must use his intelligence to not just 'offer assistance to negotiate a settlement', he must demand he assist to negotiate a settlement?

But first, Xi must fix his own performance inside China. His harsh 'one-man' leadership style to suppress Covid-19 seems to have lost support of many Chinese, the property market meltdown in which China's landscape is dotted with half-built apartments means many families will never get a home; the treatment of Uyghurs has raised persistent doubts; and then there is Taiwan. All these are not encouraging signs that Xi's promise in the 14th Five-year Plan to construct "a secure, stable and peaceful China" in all respects by 2035 is still on track.

As Albert might observe, if spiritual reform is the capping stone of China's long-term objective to join the global community of nations, as the Five-year Plan and strategy 2035 say, then Chinese people have to find the way to get it back on track. "It is of extreme importance, not for China alone, but for the whole world, in which direction they will turn for inspiration and help."[169]

Chapter 12:   LOOKING FORWARD

OF deep intellectual integrity who recognized the foolishness of their respective generations, Albert and Ben each tried, humbly and quietly, but with extraordinary perseverance and dedication, to open the eyes of the blind. Both thought a lot about the future and did remarkable things for their and future generations.

An inspired teacher of what makes the Earth's climate work, Ben clearly established in the World Meteorological Organization publication that human-induced rising CO_2 levels in the atmosphere was at the heart of accelerating climate change. "It has not gone unnoticed that the ups and downs in weather and climatic variability that has been recognized since 1960 have taken place at a time of phenomenal growth in world population which has given rise to speculation that human activities are now so extensive that they may be having repercussions on climatic variability on the global scale." [170]

Sixty years later, enough warning shots have been fired – repetitive 1-in-100-year storms, floods, cyclones, fires; Arctic and Antarctica warming; heat waves overlap and cluster; deforestation and the permafrost 'belching greenhouse gases into an already overburdened atmosphere', [171] that no one (individual, business, city, government, united nations) can be under the illusion of what will happen if Ben's scientific message falls on deaf ears. Earth is going to end up a living hell if we don't use our brains to create the global action needed to bring Earth's atmosphere back into balance.[172]

It depends on what we want Earth to become – Dante's inferno, purgatory or a heavenly place. Perhaps the worst-case scenario is Earth continuing to be left to its own devices – increasing population growth and continuing CO_2 accumulation, as implied in Ben's 1992 WMO report.

In 1945, Albert correctly foresaw the emergence of China as a mighty nation, but wondered what its spiritual base would be.[173]

Albert wrote how the Christian Literature Society in Shanghai developed a campaign to reach China's rulers by distribution of periodicals, books, pamphlets, and lectures showing how educational and religious development impacts on industries, trade and every area of national development. The campaign had two themes: to show "the supreme power of the moral and spiritual truths of Christianity to bring about general reformation", and to demonstrate "the need of direct enlightenment in regard to the material, social and political welfare of the people". In Albert's view, both were needed. [174]

Albert's radio broadcasts and his Bible translation and distribution across China in the mid-1930s must have contributed to the laying of a platform that resulted in China's founding communist leadership's decision to add Protestantism and Catholicism to the list of permitted religions. The standing of both across China was such that they could not be left out.

China has developed rapidly since Albert's tenure, and the potential contribution that religions may take in the years to come remains open. "The Parting of the Way" continues. As I write (through 2022), President Xi Jinping has acknowledged the importance of the spiritual dimension in a modern China, and has promised to explore the Bible for appropriate quotations for use in China's "peaceful" national development activities.[175] But whether he will be diverted from seeking to define a religion with sufficient "Chinese characteristics" that will be understood as 'good news' for all, and for the whole of every Chinese – body, mind and spirit – remains unclear. It boils down to whether China will continue to develop along a peaceful road, or divert (or be diverted) on to a warlike path on its journey towards global greatness and dominance.

Many in China appear to be atheist or still gain satisfaction from aligning to a range of traditional 'folk' religions. Is China's adoption of Protestantism (and Catholicism) therefore simply a token gesture to the "West", and irrelevant to the future development of modern China? Under China's one-man (Roman-like) leadership system, can religions be eliminated if considered a potential threat to the authority that governs the modern China state?

Certainly, China must have looked west in recent years and seen the emergence of Islamic states as a threat to China's state authority. The Uyghurs may be paying a huge price to protect China's western borders from a potential Islamic threat. The excuses continue: the existence of international conflicts involving national securities, always initiated by the 'enemy', which leads us back to the need for global thinking and solutions.

Albert and Ben were far more similar than either of them acknowledged, both in terms of how they pursued their life goals and how they grappled with the imponderables of the universe and Earth's future.

That they disagreed on the 'first cause' of the universe and on the path to enlightenment is not necessarily a fundamental difference at all.

Each in his own Waldensian-like way was a seeker of the Truth, a pursuer of the Tao. Each felt they had a calling to share their intellectual and spiritual journey with others, for the mutual benefit of all. They both lived a life of balance and harmony, finding their way through life in the same way that a river flowing through the country finds its natural course. Ben pursued knowledge to the point of taking no (further) action, and yet nothing was left undone. He was content when I sat with him in Torre Pellice shortly before he died.

This is not to say he was unconcerned by the huge dangers to Earth posed by the nuclear threat, climate breakdown, the increasing population and growing waste mountains. He had sought to understand the problem and the solution – how humans use or don't use their brain. He wanted education 'about the brain' as a core subject in schools. He closed a long, active life of teaching and scientific endeavour with a vision of a future that is yet to be created.

A key point he made was that evolution had equipped us with *three* brains, each unaware of the others and each pulling us in different directions. In other words, each stage of evolution had equipped us with an additional layer to our brain, but left the earlier one(s) still functioning at a totally subconscious or unconscious level. In order for us to solve our core problem, survival of the human species, we need to recognise which of our brains is driving our various actions and reactions and know how to ignore or deal with the unhelpful and destructive messages coming from the more primitive elements of our brains.

Although I never met or spoke with Albert, over all the years of correspondence, his influence was to gradually convey an interest in a world wider than myself. I was encouraged to be flexible and adventurous, and pick opportunities that gave me a chance to learn new things and grow as a person. Think of every task not only as worthwhile in itself, but also an experience that prepares me for the next opportunity that comes along.

He communicated the idea that to become happy (and stay happy) required me to pursue my interests, give something back to my community and remain true to my values.

Without mentioning a belief in God, Albert encouraged a certain humbleness and claimed that he had much to be humble about. While he occasionally mentioned his devotion to Dante's *Divine Comedy*,[176] he never explained or gave any examples of what he meant. Perhaps, to be humble was to believe that all people are equal and deserve respect.

When I began writing this book, Albert was the catalyst. He cared enough to write to a 10-year-old grandson and nurture him into an action-led adulthood over the next 30 years. Why? That remains, perplexingly unconfirmed, other than his pride in the Garnier name and Waldensian heritage. And what an exciting, full life he led. What drove him? Clearly, he wanted more from life than being a reliable, trusting bread-winning father to a family; his mission was to 'apply the power of Christ' to heal diseases and help mankind solve the riddle of the world. He was intelligent but simple, kind but strong willed and lacked an ego, and yet what a huge ego he had to spend a working life attempting to influence the evolution of China, it turns out, one of the world's first civilized societies.

Perhaps also Albert was humbled (or humiliated) by a mixture of guilt (his own for abandoning Ben and a proxy-guilt for the fact that Ben had followed suit and abandoned his own son), together with compassion (for an abandoned child) and empathy. He knew what it was like to lose a father at a young age.

As I later read Albert's (and Ben's) papers, I was struck by two things. Albert's passionate statements of belief in God, the creator and saviour. Yet no mention of this in his letters, but instead the importance of adopting a set of values – responsibility, fairness, integrity, action – that enable a life of purpose, a life that can achieve lasting benefit and contentment.

Albert's Waldensian values came through, and some complex thinking. In pursuing humility, we help build a moral sentiment in ourselves and others. Albert lived a life wanting God's approval. His papers mention his struggle with sin and working ceaselessly at earning God's love and forgiveness. This quest for 'worthiness' was an end in itself. Little of this concern was passed to me in his letters – simply the idea of leading a worthwhile life. There was no mention of leading a life to either avoid Dante's terrors of hell or earn the eternal delights of heaven. And while he sometimes mentioned Dante, it passed over my head, and I am told he could quote whole sections of *The Divine Comedy* verbatim. [177]

Second, he never mentioned in his letters that he had been interned during World War II. Albert's account of his Isle of Man imprisonment reveals a lot about his personality – his humbleness and non-violent trust of the treatment he was 'forced' to endure, his anguish at being treated as an 'enemy alien' when he had served 30 years as a Baptist (British) missionary in China and had been recruited to serve in the Censor's office, the disregard for his patriotism, his frustration at the slowness of the bureaucracy to act. His soft, attractive personality comes through, including his ability and desire to listen to heart-felt concerns of his fellow prisoners.

The fact that his account of his internment (and much else about his life) was unknown to his family (including his children) until after he died showed, again, his humbleness and secrecy.

While Albert based his life and career in a very foreign and distant land advocating for Christianity, his son, Ben, moved in a completely different academic direction, achieving milestones in a variety of nations. Both were pioneers, one guided by religious belief, the other by scientific truth and pursuit of academic excellence.

Albert's 30 years in China and then war-torn Europe was truly transformational. For much of his life, Albert lived 'a closed society' lifestyle – growing up an heir to a very proud and noble lineage of Waldensian believers who accepted martyrdom as part of the cost of their faithfulness to 'God's truth', to living in feudal China where he experienced hate ('foreign devil'), despair (wretched poverty of many), and, after the 1911 Revolution, hopelessness (of Shanghai prisoners awaiting execution).

But Albert constantly sought freedom, for himself, for his family and for his congregation. He established a China-wide radio station able to broadcast religious programmes to a listening audience of millions, translated the Bible and other Western books into popular Chinese, set his family free from the burdens of missionary life in China, and wrote many sermons and delivered them with a passion and strong insights into his core beliefs about God.

Following his return to Britain, it must have been a humiliating, anguished time behind barbed wire on the Isle of Man during the war years. It was as if the 'enemies' of the open society had pressed on him a fear of the unknown. He embraced religion with a sense of Dante's *Inferno* awaiting him.

In his later years, he enjoyed the freedom to travel between Italy, Switzerland and England and, from 1949 to 1972, was the enthusiastic (and much-loved) pastor to the Huguenot Congregation weekly service in French in the Crypt of Canterbury Cathedral.

Ben, in contrast to Albert, was flexible in pursuing a career that gave him opportunities to learn new things and grow as a person. He thought of every position he held not only as being worthwhile in itself, but also as being an experience that would prepare him for the next opportunity that came along. In this way, he became adaptable, enjoyed himself and became successful – travelling from England to New Zealand, to Nigeria then United States and Canada. Although of Waldensian and Italian heritage, it wasn't until his retirement in 1982 that he experienced living in the Waldensian village of Torre Pellice – and then only because, as he put it, for the peace of mind created by his third wife Vanna.

Ben lived for the open society, based on Karl Popper's 'unended' *Open Society and its Enemies*, but recognized the transformation that the world had gone through in moving from the Third to the Fourth Industrial Revolution – or as he preferred to term it, the Evolution of the Earth brought about through the application of scientific findings.

Over the past few centuries learning and discovery based on science and knowledge have dominated over the domain of belief and faith to the degree that many now question the role and need for religion in the modern society.

From his research, Ben knew that it was the Greeks who started a great evolution in mankind's existence, that China played a key role in the pre-Renaissance, and that it seems, we are still in the beginning of the (full) transition from the closed to the open society. Our brain is still evolving, but mankind is poised to make stunning progress or relapse, again, as China did after the 1400s and Europe in the Middle Ages and mid-20th century.

Ben saw the Waldensians as a 'closed society' off-shoot from the still continuing scientific revolution (evolution?). While we can never return to the alleged innocence and beauty of the closed society, Ben sought to put aside any territorial aspirations and racial differences – i.e. move beyond old brain impulses – and use our intelligence – new brain thinking and actions – to make breakthroughs in curbing intra-nation warfare, solving mankind's influence on deforestation and CO_2 generation, managing population growth and educating the difference between rational and irrational thinking, affecting health and medicine.

If you go back to the origin of the terms "closed society" and "open society" coined by French philosopher Henri Bergson in 1932, it may be true that the Waldensians (and all other religious and/or political groups) belong to the "closed society" in that they cling to static systems of belief or behaviour (whether God-given or man-made), which can be deliberately or accidentally exclusive or non-inclusive. But it can be argued that in Albert's case, while he may have clung to his belief in a settled God-given set of principles, he was remarkably open-minded in many respects and closer to Ben's (and my own) liberal, dynamic openness than maybe I give him credit for.

In Gisborne I had no family story to tell. I lived without a sense of living in a good or extended family, and never invited anyone home. Thanks to my absorbing the messages in grandfather's letters and my own questioning, I gradually created a sense of my history, and built a story of my origins and a clear concept of a future 'I'. I am a Garnier and can trace my family through Ben, Albert and others back to 1265 and further back to Lyon, France. I was able to move beyond a 'closed' preoccupation with my worldview based on the immediate needs and wants of the now.

I can see that Ben and Albert had a similar struggle. Ben in particular through his study of scientific findings understood that humans had evolved to an extent where 'their' consciousness had needs and desires that are critical for survival and wellbeing as food and shelter. When the brain of a person is focused only on the immediate pain, there is hopelessness. When there is a sense of 'my story' being secured within a context of past, present and future, then there is hope.

Albert's and Ben's life shows a real-world portrayal of how to tell an important story – their story. They both learnt the science (art) of thinking and writing, and knew how to connect to listeners and readers. Albert helped me establish a sense of meaning and power of action to make a contribution based on my consciousness of things deserving to be told from the world around me. I got on with it. Ben sharpened my understanding of the importance of what was happening.

To close I would like to say a little about the context of what I gained from the years of correspondence with my grandfather, and the reconnection with my father when I was aged 35 after a gap of 25 years. I am now aged 82.

The more I think about it, the stranger it seems. The world is now very different to what it was in 1952 when Albert's first letter unexpectedly arrived, and yet so many of the changes that occurred happened so imperceptibly that I now take them for granted.

When I was a boy there were no televisions, no computers or internet, no regular air flights and no talk of global threats from man-made climate change or nuclear warfare. Perhaps the most important change is that there are now more than eight billion people on planet Earth compared to the 2.6 billion in 1952.

The world is far smaller. Throughout this time, while the population was rapidly increasing, the time it takes to travel was reducing. In 1939, Ben travelled to New Zealand by ship taking more than six weeks, he departed for Nigeria 13 years later by flying first to Australia, then in stages to Lagos, taking about a week. Albert's letters would take anything from seven to 10 days.

Today there are few places in the world that can't be reached within a day. And more important, internet connects people immediately. Relatives in distant countries who I knew little of in my youth, can today be emailed, zoomed and be seen and talked with in real time. Whenever a big event happens anywhere in the world, we see it on the television as it happens and discuss it with relatives and friends across continents. We live in an immediate, interconnected world.

In short, the world has changed enormously since the 1950s. We can condemn the scientists for inventing CO_2 emissions, and nuclear weapons that, if used, could turn large areas of the globe into uninhabitable deserts. And we can condemn the scientists, politicians, officials and businesses responsible for the misuse of technology that has created the climate crises that could snuff out large parts of cities and productive land.

But without the new technology and mass production it would have been impossible to feed, clothe and house the increased population. The advance of medicine has helped, and technology has improved water supply and sewerage. China has shown how quickly poverty can be overcome. Chinese eat better, are healthier and live longer, thanks to modern technology coupled with a 'caring' political decision-making.

But the global rise of the consciousness of an Earthly threat and the commitment to create new societies with a high survival value is itself a new exponential. The new world is coming while many still cling to its "old world, old brain" territorial imperatives.

No one knows how or whether we will win this race, but as humans we must act as if survival can triumph over destruction. Faith is still a necessary component of scientific-led change.

Finally, I would like to classify this book as a non-academic voyage into a future which secures the Garnier family history, and thereby the human-led Earth's future. I have analyzed the writings of Albert and Ben, concluding that both were quiet visionaries concerned about the world's future.

Ben and Albert were two loving and lovely Garnier like-minded souls, who traveled from the 12th century through life from different axes – Albert believed deeply in God and the destiny of mankind, Ben believed that helping the Earth was the way forward.

In his last 10 years, Ben daily walked the Torre Pellice hills that his father had tramped as a child, and his Waldensian forefathers had fought on to survive. He was at peace.

For Ben and Albert, the goals of society are either humanely secured or technically imposed, and rest on the assumption that revolutionary steps are taken to create a new society, which leads to the need for Earth-focused solutions. Clearly, both would agree that the United Nations is in need of reform – the world's nations aren't united on addressing the world's threats. Achieving sustainability across Earth requires the 'withering away of the state'.[178] In fact, the state has become more deeply entrenched in power, bureaucracy and performance. China is playing a waiting game? Survival ultimately requires mankind to, firstly, recognise our total interconnectedness, which the evolving (self-aware, rational) brain perceives, but which is at odds with the territorial urgings of our prehistoric brain. Secondly, to take the action required.

This book, if anything, is an invitation to a dialogue on the necessary changes and the consensus and action required by individuals and nations to make them.

ACKNOWLEDGEMENTS

MY first thanks go to Michael Garnier, a cousin more like a brother, of Bristol, who some years ago suggested a public tribute to our grandfather Albert Garnier was worth consideration. Michael had known Albert as a loving, modest and shy but caring grandfather since childhood. But, like myself, he knew little of Albert's 30 years in China, the detail of his successes and disappointments, the pain of his capture and imprisonment on the Isle of Man during World War II, nor the depth of his feeling for the Waldensian martyrs, until receiving Albert's papers in the early 1970s. Yet Albert had written his memoirs in 1936 and 1945. Michael also knew little of, but wasn't surprised at, Albert's 20-years of letters to me, Christopher and Susan, the children of his youngest son, Ben, after the breakup of Ben's marriage in 1950. That Albert should regularly write over many years to encourage grandchildren in far off New Zealand, showed not only the depth of his understanding for their situation, but his love and responsibility to try and reconnect me to the Garnier family.

Albert's story revealed his concern for the state of the world and the depth of the thinking behind it. I owe the very greatest thanks to Michael, and cousins Jenny Broadbridge and Carol Bruton, for filling in the gaps on Albert – the grandfather that I never met. Michael read the first draft and made valuable suggestions. I hope that what appears now meets his, and the family's, approval. Should any errors of fact or judgement either remain or have crept in, they are my responsibility alone.

I wish to record my thanks also to Vanna Garnier for giving access to husband Ben's papers and articles, which revealed the scope of his thinking on the importance of the brain's evolution and performance to solving the global issues mankind faces. I owe a debt to my wife Juliet, whose ability to see the larger picture, together with her eye for detail, has made an immense difference to the text. My debt to Juliet is incalculable. To my daughter Bettina Garnier, heartfelt thanks for her wisdom and encouragement to change certain key words during the writing of this book. Warm thanks also to my friend Steve Green for his encouragement and suggestions on laying out the various themes I tackled – Albert's life guided by religious belief, Ben's pursuit of scientific excellence and my own sense of need to praise them both for their contribution to mankind's progress in a family story.

Finally, I would like to thank the China Journalists Association for enabling a comprehensive and open visit to China. Warm thanks also to the staff of the Centro and Waldensian research centres in Torre Pellice who have helped my and Juliet's visits over the past 10 years and are part of this book. I wish to acknowledge the valuable assistance of Mark Webb in the completion of this book.

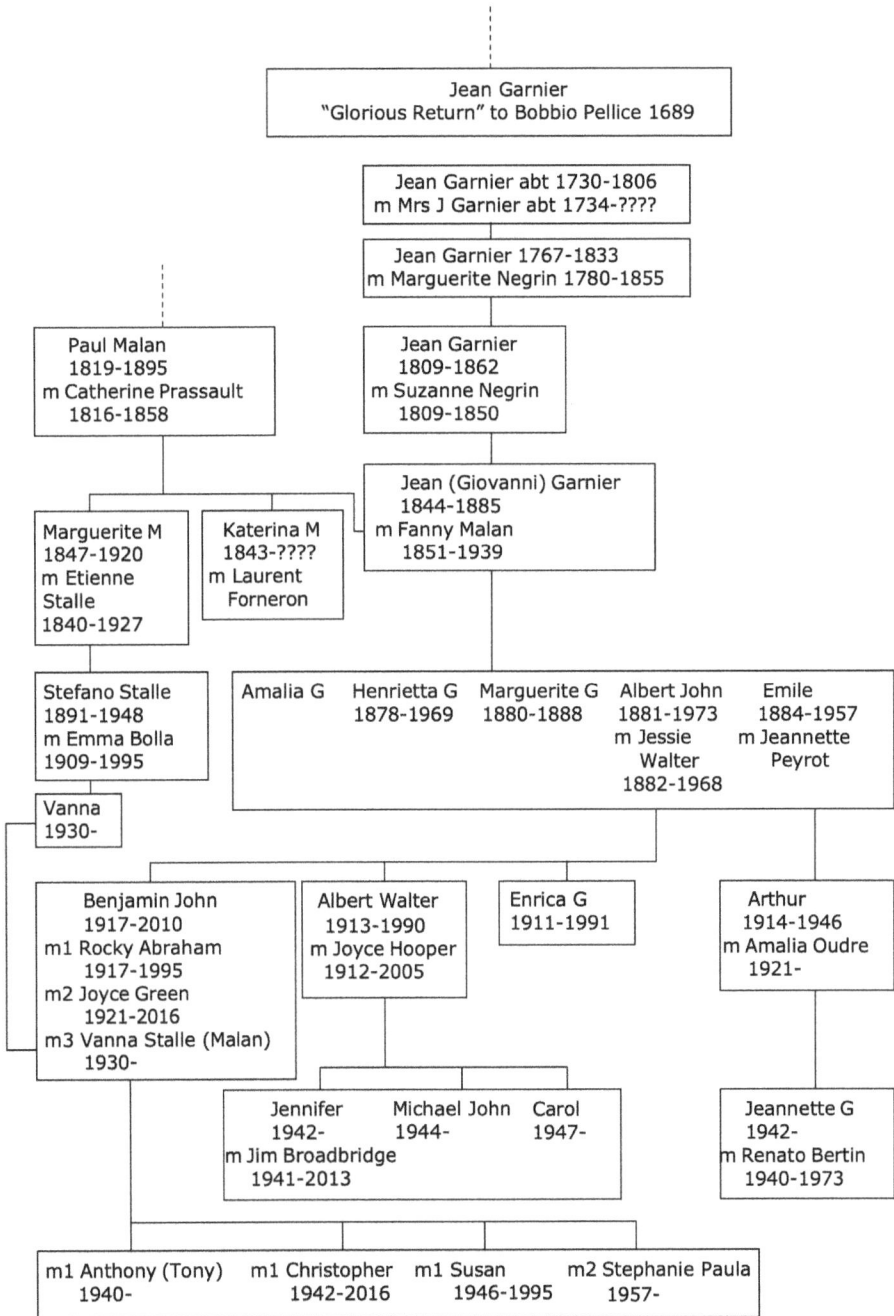

FAMILY TREE

Jean Garnier
"Glorious Return" to Bobbio Pellice 1689

Jean Garnier abt 1730-1806
m Mrs J Garnier abt 1734-????

Jean Garnier 1767-1833
m Marguerite Negrin 1780-1855

Paul Malan
1819-1895
m Catherine Prassault
1816-1858

Jean Garnier
1809-1862
m Suzanne Negrin
1809-1850

Jean (Giovanni) Garnier
1844-1885
m Fanny Malan
1851-1939

Marguerite M
1847-1920
m Etienne
Stalle
1840-1927

Katerina M
1843-????
m Laurent
Forneron

Stefano Stalle
1891-1948
m Emma Bolla
1909-1995

Amalia G

Henrietta G
1878-1969

Marguerite G
1880-1888

Albert John
1881-1973
m Jessie
Walter
1882-1968

Emile
1884-1957
m Jeannette
Peyrot

Vanna
1930-

Benjamin John
1917-2010
m1 Rocky Abraham
1917-1995
m2 Joyce Green
1921-2016
m3 Vanna Stalle (Malan)
1930-

Albert Walter
1913-1990
m Joyce Hooper
1912-2005

Enrica G
1911-1991

Arthur
1914-1946
m Amalia Oudre
1921-

Jennifer
1942-
m Jim Broadbridge
1941-2013

Michael John
1944-

Carol
1947-

Jeannette G
1942-
m Renato Bertin
1940-1973

m1 Anthony (Tony)
1940-

m1 Christopher
1942-2016

m1 Susan
1946-1995

m2 Stephanie Paula
1957-

123

BIBLIOGRAPHY

Garnier titles:

Giovanni Garnier

Ignorances et curiosities littereraires – historiques By G Garnier, Turin, Franco et fils, 1864

Collection of pedagogical maxims obtained from the best Italian and foreign pedagogues – Giovanni Garnier, Florence, Claudiana, 1875

Albert Garnier

Chinese versions of the Bible – Albert J Garnier, Christian Literature Society, Shanghai 1934

The planting of Christianity Albert J Garnier, Christian Literature Society, 1936

The Papers – A J Garnier, including 'Scenes from Imperial China,' 'Nine Letters from Tingchowfu,' 'Thirteen Letters from Shanghai', 1936 and 'An Account of my Internment at Kempton Park and in the Isle of Man', 1940, lodged in the Waldensian Library, Torre Pellice

A Maker of Modern China – Albert J Garnier, The Carey Press, 93 Gloucester Place, London, 1945

The Huguenot in Britain – A J Garnier, Black Prince's Chantry, Cathedral Crypt, Canterbury, 1965

Jessie Edith Garnier, 1882-1968: A Memoir – A J Garnier, unpublished manuscript, 1968

Early Recollections of a Missionary in China (1906-1930) Albert Garnier, published in *Le Lien*, a publication of London's Soho French church, July/August 1969

Rev A J Garnier: A Tribute – Rev H W Spillett, 1973

The Life and Papers of A J Garnier – Enrica Garnier, unpublished manuscript, 1977

Emile Garnier

Gnomonica, Orologio Solare (Theory and Practice of the Sundial), – E Garnier, Hoepli Publishers, Milan, 1939

Il Calcolo Integrale (A Calculus text book) – E Garnier, Hoepli, 1941 (various editions to 1985)

Un Po' di Calcolo Subline – E Garnier, Hoepli 1946

La Mathematica che Serve (Mathematics that serves, a practical text book) – E Garnier, Hoepli 1953 (various editions to 1990)

Ben Garnier

Articles by Ben Garnier in *New Zealand Geographer*, in Vol 1, 3, 4, 5, 7, 14; *The Professional Geographer*, Vol 15; *Weather*, Vol 9

Geography for post-primary pupils – B. J. Garnier, NZ Council of Educational Research, 1944

The Face of Otago – B. J. Garnier, Whitcombe & Tombs Ltd, Dunedin, 1948

New Zealand Weather and Climate: A Special Publication of the NZ Geographical Society – B J Garnier, Whitcombe & Tombs Ltd, 1950

The Climate of New Zealand: A Geographic Survey – B J Garnier, Edward Arnold Ltd, London, 1958

Delimiting the Humid Tropics – B J Garnier, Member if the IGU Special Commission on Humid Tropics, ICSU Review, 1960, No. 1, pages 210-218

A Program for Physical Geography – B J Garnier, Indiana University, USA, The Professional Geographer, Vol. XV, July 1963, No. 4, pages 16-18

Practical Work in Geography – B J Garnier, Prof. of Geography, Indiana University, USA, Edward Arnold (Publishers) Ltd, London, 1963

Weather Conditions in Nigeria – B.J. Garnier, *Climate Res. Series, No.2, McGill Univ., 1967*

The McGill University Climatology Programme in Barbados – B J Garnier, Prof. of Geography, McGill University, The American Meteorological Society, Vol. 49, No.6, June 1968, pages 636-639

A Method of Calculating the Direct Shortwave Radiation Income of Slopes – B J Garnier and Atsumu Ohmura, McGill University, Journal of Applied Meteorology, Vol. 7, No. 5, October 1968, pages 796-800

The Evaluation of Surface Variations in Solar Radiation Income – B J Garnier and Atsumu Ohmura, McGill University, Solar Energy Society Conference, 1968

A Viewpoint on the Evaluation of Potential Evapotranspiration – B J Garnier, Professor of Geography, McGill University, Montreal, Publications in Climatology, Vol. 25, No. 2, pages 13-24

Maritime Microclimatology: The Radiation Balance of East-Facing Slopes in Barbados – Final Report, Department of the Navy, Office of Naval Research, Geography Branch, Washington D.C., March 1975

An Approach Towards Formulating Procedures for Developing Topoclimatic Indices – B J Garnier, Climatological Bulletin No. 31, McGill University, April 1982

Compendium of Lecture Notes in Climatology for Class III and Class IV Personnel – B J Garnier, World Meteorological Organization, Geneva; WMO No. 726, 1992

Tony Garnier

The Hunter & The Hill: New Zealand Politics & the Kirk Years – Tony Garnier (co-author), Cassell New Zealand, 1978

The Parliamentary Press Gallery – Tony Garnier, article in "Politics in New Zealand, edited – Stephen Levine, George Allen & Unwin 1978

Election '81: An End to Muldoonism? – Tony Garnier (co-author), Methuen New Zealand, 1981

A China Trip – Tony Garnier, 1987, five articles based on a visit to China. See National Library of New Zealand (plus other international articles)

Auckland Voice of Business: A History of the Auckland Chamber of Commerce 1856-2006 – Tony Garnier, Auckland Regional Chamber of Commerce, 2006

Auckland Regional Economic Profile – Tony Garnier, for Auckland Regional Enterprise Board, Snedden & Cervin Publishing, 1992

Business Auckland: The definitive guide to doing business in the investment capital of the South Pacific – Tony Garnier, Nahanni Publishing Ltd, 1998

Other titles

The Glorious Recovery by the Vaudois (Waldensians) of their Valleys – Henri Arnaud, John Murray, London 1827; Reprinted by Albert Meynier, Torino 1988

Erewhon – Samuel Butler, Penguin Books 1935, first published 1872

Philosophical Dictionary – Francois Voltaire, Penguin Books, 2004, first published 1874

The Israel of the Alps: A Complete History of the Waldenses of Piedmont and their Colonies – Alexis Muston, Blackie, London, 1875

Myths & Legends of China – E T C Werner, George G Harrap & Co 1922

Science and Civilisation in China – Joseph Needham, especially the third volume of dealing with mathematics and astronomy, published 1959

Physics and Philosophy – The Revolution in Modern Science – Werner Heisenberg, Penguin Books 1962

Lao Tzu – Tao Te Ching – D C Lau (Translator), Penguin Books 1963

The Birth of Communist China – C P Fitzgerald, Penguin Books 1964

The Glass Curtain Between Asia and Europe – R Iyer (Editor), Oxford University Press 1965

The Triune Concept of the Brain and Behaviour – Paul D. MacLean, University of Toronto Press, 1973

Unended Quest – Karl Popper, Fontana/Collins 1974

La Pietra e la Voce – (The Rock and Voice), Guido Odin, published by Claudiana, Torino 1974

Escape from Evil – Ernest Becker, The Free Press, Macmillan & Co., 1975

The Human Brain – M. C. Wittrock (and others), Prentice Hall, 1977

Janus – A Summing Up – Arthur Koestler, Hutchinson & Co 1978

The Brain – The Last Frontier – Richard M. Restak, Doubleday, 1979

Build Socialism with Chinese Characteristics – Deng Xiaoping, Foreign Languages Press, Beijing 1985

The Machinery of Nature – Paul R. Erlich, Simon & Schuster 1986

The Cult of Information – Theodore Roszak, Pantheon Books, 1986

Immortality – Milan Kundera, Faber & Faber Ltd 1991

Voice of the Earth – Theodore Rozak, Simon & Schuster, 1992

The Waldensian Story: A Study in Faith, Intolerance and Survival – Prescot Stephens, Book Guild Publishing Ltd 1998

No Death, No Fear – Comforting Wisdom for Life – Thich Nhat Hanh, Riverhead Books 2002

The Future of Life – Edward O Wilson, First Vintage Books 2003

Frida and Her Brothers: The Malan Family in the Resistance – Piera Egidi Bouchard, Claudiana Publications 2003

1434: The Year a Magnificent Chinese Fleet Sailed to Italy and Ignited the Renaissance – Gavin Menzies, HarperCollins 2008

Bomb, Book and Compass – Joseph Needham and the Great Secrets of China – Simon Winchester, Viking 2008

God is Back: How the Global Revival of Faith is Changing the World – John Micklethwait & Adrian Wooldridge, Penguin 2009

What Chinese Want – Culture, Communism, and China's Modern Consumer – Tom Doctoroff, Palgrave Macmillan 2012

The Sixth Extinction – an Unnatural History – Elizabeth Kolbert, Bloomsbury 2014

The Waldenses Yesterday and Today – David Cloud, Way of Life Literature (fbns@wayoflife.org) 2015

Charles Brasch – Journals 1945-1957 – Peter Simpson (Editor), Otago University Press 2017

The Waldensians: A story of Faith and Survival – Kathleen M Demsky, A paper presented for the 9th Annual Celebration of Research and Creative Scholarship, 2017

A Communist in the Family – Searching for Rewi Alley – Elspeth Sandys, Otago University Press 2019

A House in the Mountains – The Women Who Liberated Italy from Fascism – Caroline Moorhead, Vintage 2020

The Future We Choose – Surviving the Climate Crisis – Christiana Figures & Tom Rivett-Carnac, Manilla Press, London 2020

Most of the unsourced quotes attributed to Albert Garnier come from "The Papers" he compiled in 1936, 1940 and 1945. These are unpublished but a copy is lodged in the Waldensian Library, Torre Pellice.

Endnotes

Prologue

1   Gisborne is situated at 178*E, just 2 degrees from the GMT longitude line running around the world through Greenwich, London.

2   Values confirmed by the Waldensian Synod 1974: Evangelization, economical poverty, critical freedom compared with every absolute religious-political system, freedom of the Spirit, community character of Christian (Protestant) life.

3   Extract from Albert's letter, 21st September, 1968:

你的中文求信使我最有快樂
現在我本人已是年老的，所以
常有跟不上新時代的危險。
生活在已往的時代。但是過
去的不能再同來。今天才是
我們所有的一天。不知道你
現在今還是一位集郵家。
我集郵票的機會今日不大，
可是還願意研究我所有
的中國郵票，特別是中華
民國十年（一九二）第一次
發行的航空郵件目的郵票

4   See *Like YOU say YOU ARE Tired* by Tony Garnier, *Auckland Star*, December 12, 1970, p.5.

5   See Bibliography for more detail of Kirk and Muldoon books, plus China visit manuscript

6   See *The Evening Post*, 30 November 1981. The 1981 Election saw the governing National Party, led by Robert Muldoon since 9 July 1974, win a third term in office, but the opposition Labour Party, led by Bill Rowling, won the largest share of the votes cast.

7   See *New Yorker*, Sept 26, 1977. An expression of "querencia" in one person is likely to set up a similar vibration in another, even if the other's home is on the

opposite side of the globe. Separation most effectively enlarges the meaning of "querencia"; Away from neighbourhood, away from region, away from nation, we become aware of neighbourhood, region and nation as objects of "querencia".

Chapter 1

8   Taiyuan is an ancient city with more than 2500 years of urban history, dating back from 497 BC. It was the capital or secondary capital of numerous dynasties. The two Chinese characters of the city's name are 太 (tài, "great") and 原 (yuán, "plain"), referring to the location where the Fen River leaves the mountains and enters a relatively flat plain. Its strategic location and rich history make Taiyuan one of the economic, political, military, and cultural centers of Northern China

9   See Philosophical Dictionary, by Voltaire, 1764.

10   Following the Opium Wars of 1842-44 and 1858-60, China was opened to Westerners. Although there had been a Jesuit mission in China since the 16th-century, the arrival of Christianity in force, including Protestant missionaries of the Baptist faith, had a profound impact on Chinese culture and history. The Taiping Rebellion (1850-64) which nearly toppled the Qing (Manchu) dynasty and took an estimated 2-30 million lives, was led by Hong Xiuquan, who was influenced by Christian teachings and thought that he was Jesus' younger brother. The Boxer Rebellion (1899-1900) brought death to thousands of Chinese Christians and several hundred missionaries. Yet Protestant schools, colleges, and hospitals offered educational opportunities and attracted Chinese youth. With the fall of the Qing dynasty in 1911-12, Sun Yat-sen, a Protestant favouring parliamentary government, became the provisional president. The Protestant involvement in China, particularly in education, was significant. In 1949, when the People's Republic of China was formed, Protestants and Catholics represented only one percent of the Chinese population, but as we shall see they exercised an influence out of all proportion to their size.

11   See Chung Kuo – China, the Michelangelo Antonioni documentary. Also, from "Early Recollections of a Missionary in China (1906-1930)" as published in Le Lien July/August 1969, a publication of London's Soho French church, edited by Francois Dubois, pastor of the Huguenot Crypt at Canterbury Cathedral (1967-1991), succeeding Albert who was pastor for 18 years from 1949-1967.

12   "Boxers" was a term coined by American Christian missionaries to refer to the athletic young men, because of the martial arts and weapons training they practiced.

13   See 'Taiyuan massacre' in Wikipedia.

14   The custom of separating men and women in Christian churches no longer existed in the Beijing churches and other large cities where foreign influence had already penetrated, but in the interior of China, it remained right up to the revolution of 1911.

15   See Chapter five: On a visit to China's western province of Jinjiang in 1987, I was hosted at a 12-course dinner that included chicken wings. The bones were thrown from the table into a fireplace and concrete floor nearby. I complied.

16   To Albert, Jessie (born at Blackheath, London 1882, died at Sevenoaks,

Kent 1968) was a woman for whom nothing was impossible. In a 1968 tribute he cites the painful but level headed decision for her to return to England in 1925 with their three children, beginning a separation which continued until 1937. Albert's tribute included an account of Jessie climbing Torre Pellice mountains in 1912, going over the Col du Pis (2600m) from Pragela to St. Germain and Fournasa; and over the Col de la Gianna (2525m), after having crossed the Col des Traversettes (2925m) and set foot in France. As they walked, "the thought of the old Waldenses besieged at the Bastille by the French Army under the famous general Catinat haunted me. I could almost hear them singing the psalm 'Faut-il, grad Dieu, que nous soyons epara'. As I looked at Jessie tramping along by my side, I could see in her the same indomitable spirit." (See Jessie Edith Garnier (nee Walter), pages 10-11).

17   A few years later this money disappeared, when the 1911 revolution replaced the feudal economy.

18   *See Myths and Legends of China* by E T C Werner, 1922, p.28.

19   See *A Maker of Modern China* (Maker) by A J Garnier, 1945 p.18-19.

20   See Chapters 5 & 11 for an assessment of Protestantism under President Xi Jinping, and Wikipedia for an overall summary of China's religion.

21   See *Maker*, p21-22.

Chapter 2

22   See *Maker*, p.35-37

23   At the outbreak of the Revolution in 1911, Yuan Shikai had control of the Army, making him an important figure; as a consequence, he was courted by both the Qing and the Republicans. In late 1911, Shikai commanded his army in battle against republican revolutionaries. However, a week later, he changed sides after being offered the presidency in a post-Qing republican government and was sworn in as president in February 1912, a position he held until 1916. See 'Yuan Shikai' on Wikipedia website for more details.

24   "Drosky": An open four-wheeled horse-drawn carriage formerly used in Russia and Poland.

25   See *Maker*, p91

Chapter 3

26   See Taiyuan University of Technology website: With a history of 100 years and a policy to "Pursue Practicality, Create Originality, Serve Locality", it is now a modern general university, which is majored in engineering, conjoined by engineering and sciences, and harmonized with many other disciplines.

27   Albert's other two children, Enrica and Wallie were at boarding school in Beijing (Peking).

Chapter 4

28   See *Maker*, p.64. The 12-Year programme can perhaps be regarded as a predecessor to the rolling '5-year plan' announcements eventually adopted by the Chinese government

29   See *Maker*, p.72-79

30   See the titles still available at the Chinese Christian Literature Council, successor to the C.L.S.

31   David Cairns (1862-1946) was a minister of the United Presbyterian Church who became actively involved with many public movements, including speaking tours in the United States and China.

32   Giovanni Papini (1881-1956) was a controversial journalist, essayist, novelist, short story writer, poet, literary critic and philosopher who through a lengthy career championed positivism, idealism, pragmatism and futurism before eventually settling on Christianity. He felt a strong aversion to all beliefs, to all churches, as well as any form of servitude (which he saw as connected to religion). Wikipedia state that Papini became a teacher at Bologna University in 1935, when the Fascist authorities confirmed his 'impeccable reputation' through the appointment. In 1937, Papini published a *History of Italian Literature,* which he dedicated to Benito Mussolini. When the Fascist regime crumbled in 1943, Papini entered a Franciscan convent under the name "Fra' Bonaventura".

33   *The Betrothed (I Promessi Sposi)* is an Italian historical novel by Alessandro Manzoni, published between 1840 and 1842. Manzoni hatched the basis for his novel in 1821 when he read a 1627 Italian edict that specified penalties for any priest who refused to perform a marriage when requested to do so. Set in Lombardy in 1628, during the years of Spanish rule, the novel is also noted for its extraordinary description of the plague that struck Milan around 1630. The novel deals with a variety of themes, from the illusory nature of political power to the inherent injustice of any legal system; from the cowardly, hypocritical nature of one prelate (the parish priest Don Abbondio) and the heroic sainthood of other priests (the friar Padre Cristoforo, the cardinal Federico Borromeo), to the unwavering strength of love (the relationship between Renzo and Lucia, and their struggle to finally meet again and be married). The novel is renowned for offering keen insights into the meanderings of the human mind. *The Betrothed* was made into an opera, and there have been many film versions (1908, 1941, 1990) and *Renzo and Lucia,* made for television in 2004. In May 2015, at a weekly general audience at St. Peter's Square, Pope Francis asked engaged couples to read the novel for edification before marriage.

34   See *Rev A J Garnier: A Tribute* by Rev H W Spillett. Like Albert, Spillett was a first-class Chinese linguist, and briefly a missionary in China until the outbreak of World War II. In 1947, he returned to China and served there until 1952. In the following year he was seconded to Hong Kong to work with the Chinese Christian Literature Council, serving as General Secretary until retirement in 1967.

35   See Chinese Christian Literature Council website of publications between 1906 and 1993.

36   See *Maker,* p.94.

37   See *Maker,* p.95.

38   László Ede Hudec (1893 – 1958) was a Hungarian – Slovak architect active in Shanghai from 1918 to 1945 and responsible for some of that city's most notable structures. As well as the Christian Literature Society building, near the

Bund, Hudec buildings include the Park Hotel, and the Grand Theatre. Hudec studied architecture at Budapest University and as a patriotic Austro-Hungarian citizen volunteered to join the Austro-Hungarian Army after outbreak of World War I, but was captured by the Russian Army in 1916 and was sent to a prison camp in Siberia. While being transferred, he jumped from a train near the Chinese border and made his way to Shanghai, where he joined the American architectural office R.A. Curry. In 1925 he opened his own practice, and was responsible for at least 37 buildings up to 1941. After the Munich Agreement, (1938) Hudec lost his Czechoslovak citizenship and applied to become Hungarian citizen. In 1941 he obtained a Hungarian passport and was appointed Honorary Consul of Hungary in Shanghai. After leaving Shanghai in 1947 Hudec moved to Lugano and later to Rome. In 1950 he moved to Berkeley where he taught at the University of California.

39   See Rev Spillett's tribute to Albert

40   See *Maker*, p.96.

41   See *History of China's First Gospel Radio Station* translated by Nicolas Cao, Wikipedia.

42   It was a Baptist custom for individual churches to "sponsor" a missionary, hence his letters to them.

43   See *Maker*, p.93.

44   See "Bomb, Book & Compass: Joseph Needham and the Great Secrets of China, by Simon Winchester, Viking 2008, p.113. Winchester reports that Rewi Alley, the most famous New Zealander ever to live in China, came up with the guerrilla industry scheme: Alley bicycled, walked and hitchhiked for thousands of miles across China attracting volunteers, setting up plants, and then moving on.

45   A reference to the rise of Hitler and the Nazis.

Chapter 5

46   See Chapter 11.

47   See *Maker*, p.87.

48   See *Maker*, p.116.

49   See *Maker*, p.96.

50   A colleague of Albert's at the BBC, Hsiao Ch'ien reported back to China about the European war and the war effort of the English.

51   See *Maker*, p.117.

52   In 1949, nearing the end of the civil war, the CCP established the People›s Republic of China in Beijing, while the KMT-led ROC moved its capital several times from Nanjing to Guangzhou, followed by Chongqing, then Chengdu and lastly, Taipei. The CCP emerged victorious and expelled the KMT and ROC government from the Chinese mainland. The ROC later lost control of Hainan in 1950, and the Dachen Islands in Zhejiang in 1955. It has maintained control of Taiwan.

53   Letter to Tony Garnier, September 1968.

54   See *Maker*, p.89.

55   See *A China Trip* by Tony Garnier, National Library of New Zealand, April 1987. The visit was made at the invitation of the China Journalists Association.

Chapter 6

56   From documents provided by Torre Pellice library.

57   Catharism was a Christian dualist movement between the 12th and 14th centuries which thrived in northern Italy and southern France. Followers were described as Cathars and are now mainly remembered for a prolonged period of religious persecution by the Catholic Church, and which succeeded in eradicating it by 1350. Cathars believed in two gods – a good God was the God of the New Testament, creator of the spiritual realm, whereas the evil God was the God of the Old Testament, creator of the physical world whom many Cathars identified as Satan. The Catholic Church asserted this was antithetical to monotheism, a fundamental principle that there is only one God, who created all things visible and invisible.

58   See *The Waldensians: A Story of Faith and Survival* by Kathleen M Demsky, 2017, p.2.

59   See Google 'Pra Del Torno' for location.

60   'Barbas' means 'uncle' to distinguish Waldensian preachers from the Catholic 'father'.

61   Waldo's pilgrimage to Italy was from Lyon, from where the Garnier's came (family belief).

62   See *Lyon History – French Moments*; https://frenchmoments.eu/lyon-history/ pages 8-9.

63   Waldensian communities were organized on two levels: first, there were the "perfect" *or* "Babas" who followed the three monastic vows of *poverty, chastity,* and *obedience,* and were itinerant preachers; and, second, the simple faithful, who were called "friends" or "known". All Waldensians could, and did, memorize entire Gospels and other parts of the Bible that Waldo had translated into the various popular languages. (See Wikipedia for more).

64   See Google Maps for a trek on the "glorious repatriation" route from Pragelato to Bobbio Pellice.

65   See Muston's history of the Waldensians.

66   Letter from Chris Garnier, 8 Dec 1965.

67   Pastor Jean Léger, a Waldensian leader and friend of Janavel, in his account of the 1655 events, claims to have known Bartolomeo Jahier closely and presents him as a "great captain, certainly worthy of memory, especially since he has always shown great zeal for the support of his cause, without ever proving to be shaken either by promises or threats, having the courage of a lion and yet humble as a lamb, always gave god all the praise of his victories." See 'Bartolomeo Jahier' and 'Jean Léger' in Wikipedia for more.

68   See *The Glorious Recovery by the Valdois (Waldensians) of their Valleys* by Henri Arnaud, published, by John Murray London 1827. Jean Garnier is listed

by Arnaud at p. 210 as one of the 'heroes of the Glorious repatriation'.

69   Janavel died of edema in Geneva on 5 March 1690. His house, known as *la Gianavella*, exists as a museum. After passing through various owners, it was acquired by the Waldensian Evangelical Church. See 'Janavel' in Wikipedia.

70   See Henri Arnaud.

71   The Waldensians have always had a liberal bias, compared to Catholics, with positions that basically reflect an individual taking self-responsibility decisions on issues such as homosexuality, abortion, bioethics and euthanasia. The Waldensian Synod supports numerous projects in the medical field, social, cultural and humanitarian causes for refugees, immigration, protection of minors and support of the LGBT community.

72   See Chapter 9 below.

73   See *The Waldensian Review* No. 114, Spring 2009, p4.

74   On June 22, 2015, Pope Francis visited the Waldensian Temple in Turin: it was the first time that a pontiff visited a Waldensian temple. The Pope apologized on behalf of the Roman Catholic Church for the persecutions to which Waldensians had been victims over the centuries.

75   Details from Torre Pellice Library and See family tree.

76   Jean and Giovanni are respectively the French and Italian version of John.

77   See Family Tree.

78   See Family Tree.

79   San Fedele Intelvi was a comune in the Province of Como in the Italian region Lombardy, located about 60   kilometres north of Milan and about 15 kilometres north of Como, on the border with Switzerland. On 1 January 2018 it was merged with Casasco d'Intelvi and Castiglione d'Intelvi to form the new comune of Centro Valle Intelvi.

Chapter 7

80   From *Answers to the Questions for Candidates for Mission Service* by Albert John Garnier, Question 1, 15 May 1906.

81   Giosue Carducci was an Italian poet, critic, scholar, and orator, winner of the Nobel Prize for Literature in 1906, highly influential literary figure in his time. Carducci was regarded as the unofficial national poet of modern Italy, and was anti-Catholic. His famous anti-Vatican poem 'Hymn to Satan' (1865), a worship of nature, rationalism, and the goods of life, was fiercely condemned in the clerical and conservative journals.

82   Letter from Chris Garnier, December 1965.

83   **"Vin cuit" is a dessert wine** made by heating grapes so the juice becomes syrupy. The alcohol content is around 1.4%.

84   It is significant that the female side of the Garnier family gets so little mention or credit for the key role it has played. Women like Fanny, Henrietta, Enrica, Jessie, Vanna, Juliet, Sue and others are all incredibly influential in the way the "Garniers" have performed in their profession and yet they remain largely invisible and unsung. They had/have strong personalities and equal status

in their relationships with partners but invariably deferred to the patriarchal model of family. Enrica, for example, expressed to me her strong support for the male Garniers and keeping the line going. See Albert's Tribute to Jessie.

85   During World War I, Emile was in the Italian Alpine Troops – see Chapter 11.

86   See *La Matematica Che Serve* by Emile Garnier, published by Hoepli, Milan, 1930. *The Mathematics You Need* was published in seven editions (up to 1990) for use by middle and vocational schools and technicians of all arts and industries covering algebra, trigonometry, and analytical geometry as a work tool in schools, workshops, and construction sites.

87   Professor Jean Jalla, taught at the Waldensian College in Torre Pellice.

88   The *Divine Comedy* written by Dante Alighieri between 1308 and his death in 1321, is widely considered the central epic poem of Italian literature, the last great work of literature of the Middle Ages and the first great work of the Renaissance. A culmination of the medieval world-view of the afterlife, it establishes the Tuscan dialect in which it is written as the Italian standard, and is seen as one of the greatest works of literature. The Divine Comedy is composed of three sections – Inferno (Hell), Purgatorio (Purgatory), and Paradiso (Paradise).

89   See *Israel of the Alps* by Alexis Munster.

Chapter 8

90   See *Geography for Post-primary Pupils* by B. J. Garnier, NZ Council of Educational Research, 1944.

91   Ken Cumberland, became a long-serving Professor of Geography at Auckland University.

92   See 'New Zealand Geographical Society' website: nzgs.co.nz/journals.

93   See *Compendium of Lecture Notes in Climatology for Class III and Class IV Personnel* prepared by B. J. Garnier, for Secretariat of World Meteorological Organization, Geneva, WMO-No. 726, p.55, 1992.

94   See Eltham School magazine, 1934.

95   Email from Michael Garnier 2022.

96   Conversation with Ben Garnier 2009.

97   See Otago University website, Otago Geography/Department of History.

98   The account noticeably makes no mention of pre-1848 'human' settlement – Maori, whalers and sealers.

99   See *The Face of Otago* by B J Garnier, p61.

100   See *The Face of Otago* p44.

101   See *Climate of New Zealand* map, p.35.

102   *See Climate of New Zealand* p14.

103   According to Research professor of engineering, John Davies, McMaster University.

104   See Professor John Mather, Department of Geography, University of Delaware.

105   See McGill University *Climatological Bulletin* website. In 1983 the Bulletin was taken over by the Canadian Meteorological and Oceanographic Society.

106   Two reports, in 1971 and 1975, into the energy budget and microclimate of Barbados for the Department of theNavy, Office of Naval Research, Washington, D.C.

107   J Brian Bird, chair of the Department of Geography, McGill, at convocation of Emeritus Professorship on Ben Garnier, 24 November 1982.

108   See WMO-No. 726, 1992

109   See WMO-No. 726, 1992, p.55

110   The United States National Oceanic and Atmosphere Administration's (NOAA's) measurements in May 2022 of carbon dioxide at the mountaintop observatory on Hawaii's Big Island averaged 420.99 parts per million (ppm), an increase of 1.8 ppm over 2021. Other scientists who maintain an independent record, calculated a monthly average of 420.78 ppm. "The science is irrefutable: humans are altering our climate in ways that our economy and our infrastructure must adapt to," said NOAA Administrator Rick Spinrad, Ph.D. "We can see the impacts of climate change around us every day. The relentless increase of carbon dioxide measured at Mauna Loa is a stark reminder that we need to take urgent, serious steps to become a more Climate Ready Nation."

111   See WMO-No. 726, 1992, Annex A5.3, p.162-163.

112   See Paris Agreement goal to limit global warming to well below 2, preferably to 1.5 degrees Celsius, compared to pre-industrial levels.

113   See WMO-No.726,1992, Annex A3.2, p.138.

114   Letter to Tony Garnier, Dec 26, 1973.

115   Enrica was engaged to British poet Norman Nicholson for more than ten years – See 'The Whispering Poet,' by Kathleen Jones.

116   See Charles Brasch, Journals, 1945-1957, published by Otago University Press, 2017, page 335.

117   See Brasch, op. cit., p.363.

Chapter 9

118   An Italian writer and poet, 1893 – 1958, Lorenzo spent the post-war years between England, France and Switzerland devoted to his writings in verse and prose. He won the Bagutta Prize in 1958. Described as having a shy temperament, he was dazed by the ceremony when receiving the award. See Wikipedia 'Lorenzo Montano'.

119   Bruno Revel, 1895-1959, was best known for his translation in 1932 from German into Italian of *Little Man, What Now?*–a novel by Hans Fallada on a little man in the Weimar Republic and which depicts the society of that time.

120   The Risorgimento Era, was a liberal movement supporting the unification and independence of Italy, which was achieved in **1870**. With French aid, the Austrians were driven out of northern Italy by 1859, and the south was won over

by Garibaldi. Voting resulted in the acceptance of Victor Emmanuel II as the first king of a united Italy in 1861.

121   The 'Arandora Star' was a 15,200-tonne ship, which belonged to the Blue Star Line, a London, based company. She was a leisure cruiser before World War II and had journeyed to almost all the oceans of the world on her many cruises, but when the war began, she was taken over by the British War Ministry and used as a troop carrier and for the evacuation of civilians from Europe and the Mediterranean. In 1939 the Arandora Star evacuated a boatload of women and children from the island of Malta. She was also used to take Canadian troops to Britain to help with the war effort.

122   See Enrica Garnier, *The Life and Papers of A. J. Garnier* 1977, (unpublished manuscript), p.40.

123   A letter from Mike Garnier, Bristol, to the Guardian on the 200th anniversary of the paper's founding in 1821: *In June 1940, my grandfather, an Italian-born Baptist minister of a church in Bromley, was arrested and interned on the Isle of Man as an "enemy alien". Along with a great many of his fellow internees, his arrest and imprisonment without any form of trial or interrogation made him question the basis for his love of Britain and support for this country, and caused him to wonder if his belief in British "justice" had been misplaced. Six months after his release, he wrote a fascinating (unpublished) account of his experiences of life as an internee, which includes the following: "We eagerly scanned all the papers for news about our prospects of release. The Manchester Guardian and the News Chronicle were favourites, for they had taken up our cause … we felt that all was not lost when it was still possible for anyone to take up the cause of 'enemy aliens' in the way in which these papers did." I offer this as further support for the Guardian newspaper, as it so rightly celebrates its bicentenary this year.* - Mon 10 May 2021.

124   Eleanor Rathborne (1872-1946) was an independent British MP who was a long-standing campaigner for women's rights & social justice.

125   Translation: "Here, you have to try anything".

126   Enrica Garnier's unpublished manuscript, p43.

127   The Armistice was signed in Sicily on 3 September 1943 and made public on 8 September between Italy and the Allies. Germany moved quickly by freeing Benito Mussolini, and most of Italy was occupied by German troops, who established a puppet state, the Italian Social Republic.

128   "Vaudois" is French for "Waldensian". See a *A House in the Mountain* by Caroline Moorehead, Vintage, 2019, p.43.

129   As described in *A House in the Mountain* in early 1944, with snow still around, the Germans were losing patience with the disruptive and increasingly effective partisans. After a partisan band attacked a barracks of frontier guards in Bobbio Pellice, the Fascists, who had a radio, summoned help and 140 soldiers arrived. Though outnumbered and having only rifles and one machine gun, the partisans managed to kill 12 Fascists and wound many more. The battle lasted all afternoon. Believing there were many more partisans, the enemy withdrew,

leaving behind prisoners and ammunition and mortars. But in Torre Pellice they took 40 hostages, including the Catholic Priest, the Waldensian pastor and several professors from the college, announcing that they would be released only if their own men were exchanged. Malan negotiated a deal; the prisoners were exchanged. At the day's end, there was just one dead partisan, but several civilians had lost their lives in the battle.

Chapter 10

130   Michael Garnier email, 2022.

131   See *The Hare and the Tortoise* by David Barash, Viking Penguin, 1986, p. 183.

132   A different kind of being, with different mental processes, might well proclaim a universe working in a different way and with different 'physical laws'.

133   See *Janus: A Summing up* by Arthur Koestler; plus *Bricks to Babel* pps 680-685.

134   See *Janus*, p. 274.

135   See *Janus*, p.8.

136   See *Janus*, p.10.

137   See *The Sixth Extinction: An Unnatural History* by Elizabeth Kolbert, Bloomsbury 2014, pages 2 and 268.

138   See *Janus*, p. 277.

139   See Needham's third volume of *Science and Civilisation in China* dealing with mathematics and astronomy, published in 1959.

140   See *1434: The year a Magnificent Chinese Fleet Sailed to Italy and Ignited the Renaissance* by Gavin Menzies, Harper Collins, 2008, for a popular account of how Chinese influenced Europe's 'age of discovery'.

141   See Werner, *Myths and Legends of China* p.55. He adds: "Their medicine was much hampered by superstition, and perhaps more so by such beliefs as that the seat of the intellect is in the stomach, that thoughts proceed from the heart, that the pit of the stomach is the seat of the breath, that the soul resides in the liver, etc – the result partly of the idea that dissection of the body would maim it permanently during its existence in the Otherworld."

142   See *Janus*, p.275.

143   See *The Dialogue between Asia and Europe* by Joseph Needham, p. 292, in *The Glass Curtain Between Asia and Europe* edited by Raghavan Iyer, Oxford University Press, 1965.

144   For Popper: An open society is associated with cultural and religious pluralism; it is always open to improvement because knowledge is never completed but always ongoing: "if we wish to remain human, then there is only one way, the way into the open society ... into the unknown, the uncertain and insecure". In the closed society, claims to certain knowledge and ultimate truth lead to the attempted imposition of one version of reality. Such a society is closed to freedom of thought. In contrast, in an open society each citizen needs to engage in critical thinking, which requires freedom of thought and expression

and the cultural and legal institutions that can facilitate this.

145   See '*Popper*' by Bryan Magee, Fontana 1973, p.83.

146   Conversation in Torre Pellice, 2009.

Chapter 11

147   "I believe the greatest dream of the Chinese people in modern history is the great renewal of the Chinese nation," Xi Jinping in 2012, the year he took office. Zhong Guo, references the Central Kingdom, home of Han Chinese.

148   For example, the Yongle Encyclopedia & Dunhuang manuscripts.

149   See China's 14th Five-year Plan, Article 111, Section 1: Long-term Goal for 2035.

150   See *What Chinese Want* by Tom Doctoroff, Palgrave Macmillan, p. 250.

151   See *Build Socialism with Chinese Characteristics* by Deng Xiaoping, Foreign Language Press, 1985, p. 18.

152   See the full text of the Chinese Communist Party's latest resolution on history released by the official Xinhua News Agency, adopted by the Party on November 11, 2021.

153   See the *Red Roulette: An Insider's Story of Wealth, Power, Corruption and Vengeance in Today's China* by Desmond Shum, September 2021.

154   According to China's news agency Xinhua, 11 March 2021, China's 14th Five-year Plan (2021-2025) for National Economic and Social Development and the Long-Range Objectives Through the Year 2035 is a blueprint for the world's second-largest economy as it kicks off a new journey towards fully building a modern socialist country. The drafting took three years, guided by proposals of the Chinese Communist Party Central Committee, and field work to take account of people's suggestions from all walks of life. A detailed plan was formulated and submitted to the top legislature's annual session for review and approval. Analysts say it is democracy in full swing, involving a constructive mix of top-level design and people's wisdom, both online and offline. As a system of consensus-building, it is different from that in the West – "It is quiet, and in many ways, like Tai Chi." Many great achievements have been accomplished in China in this way, including the eradication of absolute poverty.

155   See *Maker*, p116.

156   See *The Economist* 15 September, 2021.

157   See *Civilization: The West and the Rest* by Niall Ferguson, a leading historian of the global economy and author of *The Ascent of Money, The Pity of War, The Cash Nexus: Money and Power in the Modern World, Empire: The Rise and Demise of the British World Order, Lessons for Global Power*, and *The War of the World: Twentieth Century Conflict and the Descent of the West*.

158   Ian Johnson works out of Beijing and Berlin.

159   See *God is Back: How the Global Revival of Faith is Changing the World* by John Micklethwait and Adrian W Wooldridge, 2009.

160   China's Religious stats (2014): Buddhism, 15.87%; Taoism, 7.6%; Protestantism, 2.19%; Islam, 0.45%; Catholicism, 0.34%. A 2015 Gallup poll

found the number of convinced atheists in China to be 61%.

161   See *China's New Civil Religion* By Ian Johnson, NYT Sunday Review, December 22, 2019.

162   See China's 14th Five-year Plan, p.83.

163   See China's 14th Five-year Plan, p.87 and p.8.

164   See *Maker*, pps 109 -117.

165   See Guardian, 18 October 2017.

166   See *Maker*, p.116-117.

167   See *Maker*, p.111. Albert's comment is reminiscent of South Africa's Desmond Tutu's wonderful encapsulation of European missionaries (which also applies to New Zealand): "They had the Bibles; we had the land. They told us to close our eyes and pray. When we opened our eyes, we had the Bibles and they had the land."

168   Xi Jinping in 2012, the year he took office.

Chapter 12

169   See *Maker,* p.117.

170   See WMO – No. 726), p.54.

171   See *The Future we Choose: Surviving the Climate Crisis* by Christiana Figures & Tom Rivett-Carnac, Manilla Press, 2020, p. 23 and read and act on the whole book!

172   See WMO – No.726, pages 54-55.

173   See *Maker*, p.117.

174   See *Maker, p.73.*

175   See China's 14th 5-year plan.

176   A reference to Italian writer Dante Alighieri's 14th-century epic poem *Divine Comedy: Inferno, Purgatorio and Paradiso.*

177   Email from Michael Garnier, 20 March, 2022.

178   **"Withering away of the state"** is a concept coined by Friedrich Engels referring to the idea that, with the realization of socialism, the social institution of a state will eventually become obsolete and disappear as the society will be able to govern itself without the state and its coercive enforcement of the law. Or, the world becomes a 'free market' based on scientific principles (truths) for enabling mankind's sustainable survival?